Masterpiece

The Art of Discipling Youth

Paul Martin

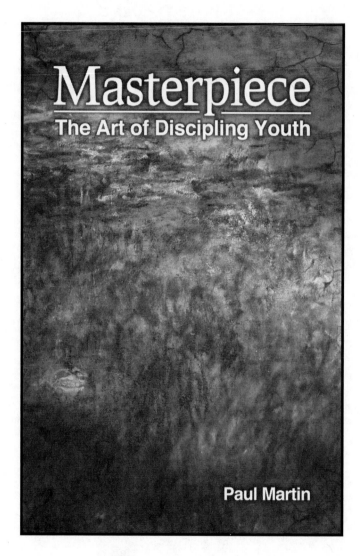

Masterpiece
The Art of Discipling Youth

Paul Martin

THE YOUTH CARTEL

San Diego, California

Masterpiece

Publisher: Mark Oestreicher

Managing Editor: Anne Jackson

Editing: Robin Pippin

Cover Design: Paul Martin

Layout: Adam McLane

Creative Director: Vinny Van Gogh

ISBN-13: 978-0-9851536-6-3

ISBN-10: 0985153660

The Youth Cartel, LLC

www.theyouthcartel.com

Email: info@theyouthcartel.com

Born in San Diego

Printed in the U.S.A.

Contents

Introduction

"All our knowledge has its origins in our perceptions."
—Leonardo da Vinci[1]

L eonardo da Vinci should have been a youth pastor. I can't think of another person in history who pursued so many different disciplines in one lifetime. Painter, cartographer, sculptor, engineer, architect, musician, mathematician, scientist, inventor, anatomist, geologist, botanist, and writer—all came from one person. Aren't youth workers asked to wear as many different hats too? Pastor, theologian, prayer warrior, teacher, counselor, arbitrator, speaker, entertainer, comedian, musician, designer, marketing guru, social networking expert, and all around merchant of cool: all characterize the prototypical youth pastor. At least that's the view of most: churches looking to hire someone to run the youth program, parents wanting a spiritual leader for their children, and youth looking for someone they can relate to.

Of all the possible fulfilling careers da Vinci could have found, he was really *just* an artist, although no one is just anything. No title can completely summarize any person, right? Da Vinci's powers of observation are what made him great. This one trait put him head and shoulders above others in many fields. Just take a look at the background of the *Mona Lisa*. The background of portraits today with its gray washes of anti-color can't touch da Vinci's eye for detail. This attention to each particular attribute shows the essential characteristic of any artist—perspective.

Perspective personalizes everything and, though it can be enhanced, it can't be taught. Most local community centers teach art classes. They cover the basic ways to appreciate art, offering techniques that painters, sculptors, and other artists use to create masterpieces. Those skills can heighten an artist's perspective, but they are no substitute for it.

This book will offer methods of discipleship, but it will only be as effective as your own ability and willingness to see. As a youth worker, you have to have the desire to look closely at young adults and see them as God's works of art, which he names all of us in Ephesians 2:10. "We are God's masterpiece," writes Paul the apostle. This book shares techniques that reveal that art in others if you are open to look closely for them.

To do this, you will refine how you see people, starting with yourself. Perspective comes from within. It highlights our unique way of viewing life. When I walk through a museum, I observe each painting, but what I really see is the artist beneath the surface. Take Monet's *Water Lilies*, for example. It conveys a sense of motion through his use of impressionism. Details run together with washes of color. Though the subject of the painting is a flower, it's the artist's take on it that gets my attention.

Discipleship

I hate to even begin this section using the "D" word, but it's in the title, so I have to address it at some point.

My editor would probably write me a nasty note if I didn't include it somewhere. I can't think of a more loaded word in the church describing as many different activities as da Vinci had career opportunities. It might mean a Bible study, small group, fellowship event, spiritual formation, or any random event held in the church. While these activities are present in discipleship, they miss its essence. For the purpose of this book, making disciples will refer to the process where one person helps to reveal God's created purpose in another, regardless of how a person may respond. It makes use of many disciplines covered very well in many wonderful books. Unlike those books, I want to guide you through several other ways that disciples grow into works of art. I don't want to paint over what is already there. Instead I want to open up disciples to the possibility that they have an identity already inside them. Taking away superimposed outcomes, responding to them instead of a pre-planned study, and allowing them to search for themselves are the foundations of discipleship. I am intent on growing your vision of guiding teenagers into practicing their faith from their core identity.

If disciples really are God's art, we can't claim much in the way of making them. No teenager arrives as a blank canvas. In making disciples, we're much more like a curator or restorer who sees the individual brush strokes making up the whole of a painting. From cutting an edge to stippling to feathering in, each touch of the bristles paints a picture. Revealing these lines often begins with cleaning mold or dirt from the face of the art. After that, cracks and peeling paint are repaired. The final step is applying a protective finish to the painting so it can be viewed once more. All of these techniques are used in revealing the original work of art. It requires a trained eye. That's very close to the art of discipling I will write about in later pages.

These steps in the process are the building blocks of what I have practiced, and what I have seen Jesus do in the lives of his followers. Like his Heavenly Father, Jesus was an artist. He could see what lay beneath the surface, as a skilled sculptor could. His sight informed the process of helping people live as God's masterpiece. Vision comes first, before any technique is necessary. As Jesus saw each person, he saw that person connected to God's hand. He could see a person's unique identity, created for a reason. Artists don't arbitrarily begin working without something in mind before they start to work.

Reading the Gospels, you might even say Jesus was a frustrated artist. How often did he offer stern correction to Peter, who just couldn't help but blurt out the first thing in his mind? Or the two brothers who sent their mother to ask favors of Jesus? Scripture implies a lot of head-shaking from Jesus. I can just imagine it as he says, "Oh you of little faith." It began many of his teachings.

Though he was the Son of God, Jesus knew he couldn't force those men to use their faith. Living as God's workmanship comes from within. Instead, he explained to them the nature of faith and how they individually were gifted to live it.

So much of Jesus' work was in chipping away all the rubble hindering each person from being God's masterpiece and from living a life of faith. Since we know Jesus was fully God and fully man, we can see examples of him as an artist. The account of creation, the inspired songbook of the Psalms, and even an analogy of God as a potter (Jeremiah 18:1-4, Romans 9:21, Isaiah 45:9) show him to be the ultimate creative. Discipleship is no different. It's art.

The practices in this book will expand your perspective and bring out details you may have yet to think about. Some of these you will have already concluded yourself. Hopefully, reading this book will affirm what you have already discovered.

Youth

When I first thought of writing this book, I didn't think it should focus on youth, though most of the practices I would write about come from my work with teenagers. These principles could be used with a person of any age. It just happens, though, that the period of pre-adulthood is the most formative time for identity to develop.

As young adults take a few steps towards independence, they look for affirmation around them about the decisions they make. Affirmation is often totally random, but weight is given to random affirmations regardless of their truth or benefit. Many teenagers become caricatures of their peers, family, or lifestyle because of these random bits of needed approval. They try on new exaggerated personas, making them seem schizophrenic at times. One day they wear Abercrombie and the next day, Hot Topic. They want to see themselves as art, but they have little direction in that discovery and even less confidence.

Youth ministry is built on the idea that each person comes to a youth group meeting for a reason. The seeds of discipleship find fertile soil in the hearts of young adults. They want to be revealed as something amazing. Youth ministry embraces this vision for teenagers. It can't help but to see the best in them and try to get them to see it for themselves.

Student ministry can be summarized in one idea: students are God's workmanship. The art of discipling them simply reveals those individual details for them and everyone else to see.

Chapter 1

Discontented: A Youth Ministry Manifesto

"Here's to the crazy ones, the misfits, the rebels, the troublemakers, the round pegs in the square holes... the ones who see things differently—they're not fond of rules... You can quote them, disagree with them, glorify or vilify them, but the only thing you can't do is ignore them because they change things... they push the human race forward, and while some may see them as the crazy ones, we see genius, because the ones who are crazy enough to think that they can change the world, are the ones who do."

—Steve Jobs[2]

Sometimes people nail it. You can see it in the proud arch of the back of an Olympic gymnast when she pulls off the perfect dismount. Somehow even the most untrained eye can tell the difference between that person and the person taking an imperceptible hop at the end. Steve Jobs nails my feelings of a new discipleship when he says, "Here's to the crazy ones, the misfits, the rebels, the troublemakers, the round pegs in the square holes... the ones who see things differently." This quote blazes in my heart.

He didn't mean it about the church or even more specifically youth ministry, but it sure is relevant. This one statement could begin a youth ministry manifesto. So it's appropriate that I start here.

Discipling youth changes them. It pushes the human race forward in ways no other work does. And yet, if you read very much about the church lately, you can't help but know something's broken.

Michael Frost and Alan Hirsch, in addressing this brokenness, refer back to the early church saying, "The church is worse off precisely because of Christendom's failure to evangelize its own context and establish gospel communities that transform the culture."[3]

Frost and Hirsch see the beginning of the downfall of the church in its institutional beginnings. Christendom set the stage for the Western church with a modern value system that organized and codified faith and its surrounding culture. By assimilating culture, it lost its mission to change it. Teens tend to resist being boxed into pre-defined roles. No wonder Steve Job's earlier statement resonates with so many people in this culture.

David Fitch also points to modernity, making a distinction between one-time faith decisions (the goal of many churches) and transformation.

> *Our churches confirm this distinction when we see an increasing disconnect between the number of decisions and corresponding life-change... an action, or for that matter a decision, is simply unintelligible separated from the rest of one's life story/narrative and one's cultural context because it is not capable of being made sense of. Apart from a context, a decision will appear to be an arbitrary act made on the spur of the moment for short-term im-mediate gain with little long-term consequences.*
> —David E. Fitch[4]

These are only a few of the ideas resonating in me through the years. I could collect more and more quotes from people who see the brokenness of the church. But don't worry; I'm not going to do that. I'll make my point here with just one more by John Eldredge.

There are few things more crucial to us than our own lives. And there are few things we are less clear about...

The cumulative effect of days upon years that we do not really understand is a subtle erosion. We come to doubt our place, we come to question God's intentions toward us, and we lose track of the most important things in life.
—John Eldredge[5]

These are the words of an artist. They are no more true than the ideas written previously, but for some reason they moved you where the others just made you feel less alone in this world. Where Fitch, Frost, and Hirsch give you details, Eldredge speaks to your heart. Your emotions as well as your mind resonate with them. While many of the claims in recent books are no doubt true about the failings of the institutional church in the west, one is absolutely crucial. The church foundered when it drifted into dispassionate pleas for knowledge and lost the voice of an artist.

As Christianity became more systematized, organized, and codified, it lost an essential trait. It melded with the culture but at some point failed to continue to shape it. I write "culture" here, but what I'm really talking about is people. Without the urgency to move people in a way that brings them closer to Christ, the church falls into one more social construct among many.

WWJD?

Have you ever thought about the way Jesus carried out his mission to the world? I don't know about you, but if it were me, I would have gone about things a little (OK, a lot) differently. Just look at the ways the church tries to fulfill the mission Jesus began. We print a lot of books, write a lot of blogs, hand out a lot of tracts, teach a lot of Bible studies, and create some really cool presentations complete with stunning visuals and ear-candied sound. I would have tried one of those approaches, or all of those approaches. But Jesus had a different way.

Jesus picked twelve men to live closely with him. These men watched what he did and then started doing the same things themselves from their own perspective. Jesus' diverse team included several fishermen, a tax collector, a doctor, an accountant, a political activist, and others. They were a cantankerous group of men making the Good Shepherd appear more to be herding cats. Each of the apostles was uniquely gifted, different in his own way. Reading about Jesus' encounters with the disciples, I wonder if there must be some omissions in translating the Bible. There just had to be some eye rolling, huge sighs of frustration, and general "whatevs" from Jesus directed at the bumblings of the disciples. Yet, Jesus used this process to fulfill his mission. He invested his life in the lives of twelve men for about three years and then let them continue the movement he started. He trusted that, in time, they would realize their purpose and understand the way they were specifically equipped to invest their own lives in others.

Jesus accomplished something amazing in the way he began Christianity, and it doesn't align closely with what the church does today. I would have picked more people. Twelve just isn't enough. What if they were all killed riding around in the church van? If I had to have just twelve, I would have interviewed hundreds, maybe thousands, and then made a selection from the best of the lot. Heck, why even go through that process when I could just have a conference with big-name speakers to equip thousands? Or maybe I would have them read lots of books and write tons of papers; but I would never have asked them to leave their work and meander around the country with me ON FOOT! Sure, my disciples might have to get up early in the morning to meet for coffee once a week: but Jesus just asked too much.

Selecting people would have looked much different as well. In picking them, I would have confirmed their acceptance privately to avoid embarrassment, had them sign contracts, and then had a formal announcement. Instead, Jesus names them publicly out of the hundreds who had been following him. Imagine the public shame of not being selected. *Ouch!* That's infinitely worse than being the last guy picked for dodgeball.

Here's the point: Jesus had a plan to continue his work after he was gone. He didn't rely on the latest Christian author or programs and events. Instead, he discipled his followers and trusted God's purpose to be revealed in each of them.

Jesus poured much more than his knowledge into them. He spent time with them, revealing their faults and abilities. Through Jesus' approach, each disciple caught a glimpse of what it was like to be God's work of art. Sure, Jesus taught the apostles; but the way he taught conveyed more than just information. He described the process of discipleship. If he hadn't revealed a way for his followers to invest this process in others, then much of his effort would have probably died 2000 years ago.

The Gospels paint for us a picture of Jesus' way of discipleship. Through this practice, Jesus showed people how to live their lives to the fullest. It was the process Jesus used to begin something that would continue for centuries.

And yet, through the ages this method has morphed

into something incredibly ineffective. By focusing on education, the church took the "remarkable" out of discipleship. It took something amazing and reduced it to small group book studies.

David Kinnaman summarizes this idea about the church,

> *We need to renew our catechisms and confirmations—not because we need new theology, but because their current forms too rarely produce young people of deep, abiding faith. We need to rethink our assumptions and we need the creativity, honesty, and vitality of the next generation to help us.*
> —David Kinnaman[6]

Discipleship's dwindling effectiveness is paradoxical because the "form" of discipleship is still there. Bible reading, praying, and fellowship are a part of discipleship, but reducing them to impersonal checklists undoes discipleship. You would think that in studying the Bible we would see Jesus' way of discipleship; yet knowledge without purpose is useless.

The Word Is a Sword

> *"Put on salvation as your helmet, and take the sword of the Spirit, which is the word of God."*
> Ephesians 6:17, NLT

The Bible compares the word of God to a sword, with the ability to cut between bone and marrow. It sounds pretty cool when you know the art of sword making. To make a traditional samurai sword, you have to know the difference between a tech manual and art. A samurai sword starts with jewel steel. It takes a continual three days and three nights of smelting over 25 tons of steel at a constant temperature of around 2500 degrees. If the flame isn't hot enough, then carbon doesn't bond to the steel, making it strong. If the temperature rises too far above 2500 degrees, then the carbon cooks out of the steel making it too brittle. Jewel steel sells for fifty times as much as regular steel.

After the steel is bonded to carbon, the swordsmith hammers it over and over again to remove its impurities. This process requires the steel to be folded hundreds of times, squeezing the slag out like water out of a sponge. Again, if the steel becomes too hot, the whole piece is ruined. Following this process produces two kinds of steel—high-carbon steel (the super-strong kind) and low-carbon steel (the softer, more malleable kind). Both high- and low-carbon steel are combined, one in the channel of the other, to make the blade. Using high-carbon steel alone makes the blade too brittle. In combat, it will crack and break. Low-carbon steel doesn't stay sharp because it's too soft. The two make a perfect blend of strength and suppleness.

After the two steels come together, the sword is covered in clay and charcoal, heated one last time to about 1500 degrees, and then dipped into water to cool it quickly. This process is called quenching, and it is essential in shaping the sword. Quenching cools the two pieces of steel at different rates. When this happens, it bends into the typical final form recognized around the world as the samurai sword. The bend is important to the slicing cut used by samurai. I've heard a straight sword doesn't have the ability to slice through bones like the samurai sword.

In ancient times, before a sword was given to a samurai, it had to make four cuts, each on a living person (or so I've heard). It had to cut through the arm at the bicep, the leg at the hamstring, the neck, and the pelvis. Each cut had to pass cleanly through the bone without breaking or dragging. If the sword made these cuts, then it could serve a samurai. If it failed any one of these cuts, it was garbage.

I could go on about swords and how they are made, describing the beauty of their hilt and scabbard, or even the special techniques used to maintain them. This would be essential if you owned one and wanted to keep it from becoming a useless piece of metal.

All of this understanding would be useless in a sword fight, though. In a battle of blades, the person with the most skill in using a sword has the advantage, not the guy who made it.

Merely teaching about the Bible and about God reduces discipleship to a knowledge factory. It ignores the skill and practice required to live the life we are created for. We will never win spiritual battles with knowledge alone. One of the many advantages of Jesus' way of discipleship was that he also made the disciples practice what they learned. To follow him, they had to rehearse the life he called them to. It became so much a part of their way of life they continued it even after Jesus left them.

Discipleship has to invest more than knowledge in its followers. James tells us that faith without works is dead (James 2:17). I have a similar saying about discipling young people: "Knowledge without purpose is dead." Teaching teenagers without a purpose wastes the opportunity to reveal God's art. Yet, the picture of youth ministries across the planet is centered around fun games, compelling worship, and teaching. Somehow, we expect teens to be able to use the knowledge given to them with little, if any, practice. If we want to see this epic victory, we have to give our disciples more than twenty minutes of knowledge a week.

The Ancient Duel

This reminds me of an obscure movie where two ancient foes square off with another. You've probably never heard of it, so I won't bore you with the title. Picture in your mind this scene: A shriveled man waddles forward. He's bent from countless years of gravity pulling against his body. Only an old gnarled stick helps him stand. He might not make it to his destination. Every step requires an effort using his last bit of strength. At each step, he plants his cane with a skill conveying years of practice.

Across the room from him stands his much younger challenger, his back straight and rigid. Clear eyes and steady hands reveal a determination to win. He reeks of readiness for the battle.

Finally, the older combatant arrives at his place and stands ready. They lock eyes, exchange a few words and then an explosion of light comes from each of their light sabers. This is the scene as the elderly Yoda faces off against the powerful Count Dooku. Previously, Yoda had been portrayed as an old, feeble monk-like character who comically has not yet mastered syntax. To the amazement of everyone watching, Yoda bursts into movement, flipping and jumping around like a gymnast who just drank ten energy drinks. He no longer looks old and bent but shows the vibrancy of a much younger warrior.

I loved seeing why they called Yoda Master for so long in the *Star Wars* movies. This scene creates a longing for me in the church. I want to see more Master Yodas. The world needs to see people who not only know the Bible, but can wield it with the agility and skill Yoda shows in this scene. In my vision of discipleship, this potential bursts forth into the kinetic realm instead of being bound to its potential in knowing.

Forming Disciplines

I'm not the only person who has realized the emptiness of knowledge without purpose. A well-known pastor wrote a book about living on purpose. He presented five purposes every believer shared. Through practicing the disciplines in this book, I grew closer to the Lord and developed a deeper relationship with him. They added a richness and depth to my life of faith. At the same time, all of the ancient practices fell short of discipleship.

Don't let this offend you if you practice spiritual disciplines. The goal of the disciplines is to bring you closer to your Creator. Discipleship shares this goal, so in a way, they are similar. However, where the disciplines focus generally on growing in relationship with God and his church, it doesn't set its goal as revealing our created identity. Much like small groups or Bible studies, this can happen through the disciplines, but it isn't the goal.

Gurus, life-coaches, mentors, spirit guides, spiritual directors and many others all understand the need for transformation. There has been an amazing resurgence of growth in the church through these people. Yet these approaches can also fall short of discipleship.

So while disciplines have a wonderful place in the Christian life, they aren't the same as the discipleship we encounter with Jesus. They can lead to that kind of relationship and are often a part of a discipleship relationship, but they alone aren't what this book is about.

Discipleship can't stop there. It studies each person and realizes his or her unique purposes as well. A disciple's unique gifting points to a hidden purpose within. Discipleship reveals it and hones it into something beautiful.

Bushido

Now, back to the swords for a minute. Ancient Japanese samurai were the masters of the sword. They dedicated their lives to serving others through a code of honor based on the life of a warrior. It benefitted feudal Japan in a time of extreme turmoil by challenging the aristocracy into a system of discipline, obedience, duty, and honor.

This life was Bushido.

It wasn't just confined to mastery of the sword. Samurai were so dedicated to this code they would end their life before being dishonored. Every samurai made his goal to have an honorable death. That's intense, but, ironically, it shows their commitment to living.

I sometimes wonder what our society would be like if Christians lived in the same way. Would it be an amazing new chapter in the Kingdom of God? Or would it be a legalism devolving into a religion of appearances? Either way, it certainly paints a great picture for people who want to learn to use the Bible instead of just study it.

Warnings

Before going any further into this idea of practicing your faith, I need to raise a couple of red flags of warning. This idea of discipleship isn't very new. You can see the results in the Bible and even afterward. Those results weren't often what most people wished for themselves. Scripture tells story after story of how a life of faith often brings contrary results. A prince becomes a nomad. A prophet marries a prostitute. Another wears a dirty girdle on the outside of his clothing. Practicing your faith in discipling others will sometimes look crazy. The people you disciple will often wonder at all of the "help" you give them. Here are a few suggestions to remember while reading this book and when practicing this kind of discipleship.

Be aware that all of the amazing things God does in a person's life are beyond you. I love solving people's problems. Some of that altruistic spirit plays a big role in discipleship, but part of me loves to be needed. If you're like me, you will need to guard yourself from trying to look wise and all-knowing. Grandstanding and playing a part reserved for the Holy Spirit only limits your effectiveness.

Be aware of what you bring into a relationship. What do you fill the room with? Some people naturally fill up empty space. It might be emotionally, intellectually, spiritually, conversationally, or even physically, but be aware of what amount space you are leaving for your disciple and for God to do his work.

You are the ceiling on experience. You can't lead people where you haven't been willing to go yourself. To work with someone, you don't have to share all of his or her experiences. But you will be less effective in challenging others if you haven't been willing to be challenged yourself.

One more thing, context guides these techniques. Like any great martial artist or jazz musician, practice only prepares you for an encounter with another. The context determines the approach used. Many discipleship skills differ and even contradict themselves when applied out of context. As you read, think about in what contexts these practices would be most useful.

Chapter 2

Process over Outcomes

"For apart from me you can do nothing."
—Jesus of Nazareth

I sat in stunned silence. It was the middle of June, and I had been called into my senior pastor's office. Remembering days in the sixth grade of being sent to the principal's office, I entered with a heart of anxiety. This visit would be nothing like the one six months previous where I was told I was exceeding expectations. Serious doesn't begin to cover the tone of this meeting.

I pretended to be a deer. *If I just stay still and quiet, nothing bad will happen*, I thought. It did anyway. My pastor had just given me my first taste of his disfavor. He told me, "I know we talk a lot about grace here, but when it comes to your job, it's performance that counts."

As I sat there stunned, I couldn't believe what he'd just said. Did he really think that church staff are so amazing that they are above the need for grace? As I tried to remember that I had a mouth and needed to respond, I wondered why he would say this. I apparently needed grace but wasn't going to get it. How could I be in such need after a glowing review only six months before? What went wrong?

As my voice returned, I frantically started asking questions. Was my "performance" not meeting his expectations? When did *that* happen? What should I do in response? As a torrent of emotions and confusion poured from me, I was given a clarifying statement from him: "If you can't change, then we will have to find someone else."

I began to realize that my employment was in jeopardy. As if that threat wasn't enough, my pastor asked me twice, "Do you still feel like you are called to youth ministry?" He was a professional athlete of motivation. After the second hearing, I realized it wasn't a question. It was a commentary on my performance.

I left our little pow-wow trying to define the meaning of performance. I was so not OK with having the expectation to always perform to someone else's standards. So in the following weeks I became an expert on what youth pastors should be able to do.

Through this process, I discovered something that changed the way I would minister to others for the rest of my life.

Up until that time, I had been taught that certain measurables brought job security. The king of these goals was conversions. Lots of teens walking the aisle meant a ministry was experiencing success. If new decisions weren't lining up, then recommitments followed in order of importance. At the very least, large groups of people smiling and having fun were required. Knowing this, I had failed to meet the expectations of my church leaders.

My way of ministry looked entirely different. Instead of smiles, I would often see tears. Reciting Bible verses only opened up more questions with teens who were trying to live out their faith. More and more, the ministry was meeting in small groups to insure a safe place to dig deeply into each teenager's life. Maybe I was performing, but to my own values instead.

Then I read something Paul the Apostle wrote a long time ago.

After all, who is Apollos? Who is Paul? We are only God's servants through whom you believed the Good

News. Each of us did the work the Lord gave us. I planted the seed in your hearts, and Apollos watered it, but it was God who made it grow. *It's not important who does the planting, or who does the watering. What's important is that God makes the seed grow. The one who plants and the one who waters work together with the same purpose. And both will be rewarded for their own hard work.* For we are both God's workers. And you are God's field. You are God's building.

—1 Corinthians 3:5-9, NLT, emphasis mine

If it doesn't matter who does the work because God makes things grow, then what was I supposed to do to plant or water? I had been pursuing an outcomes-based approach to ministry, and what I needed was to focus on the process instead.

I can't make conversions or recommitments. If our Creator changes a teen's heart and mind, then it's well out of my ability as a created being. I can't make people smile all the time either. That would be emotionally unhealthy. Imagine a teen tells you he is struggling with the death of his mother and your goal is to try to get him to smile. He needs time to grieve, not to plaster a grin across his face.

So I started to appreciate the limitations of my role as a youth pastor. Not only can I not do these things, they're not my job. Trying to force them makes it even worse. Instead of having a list of outcomes, I need to focus on the process of being faithful to God's work. Others reached the same conclusion.

When we push young people to make decisions, when we use behavior modification techniques to pressure youth to think certain thoughts and behave in "Christian" ways, we assume the role of the Holy Spirit. The problem is these practices don't lead to genuine

Masterpiece

transformation, and ultimately they do more harm than good. Mike King says this, "Too often we depend on our training, gifts and abilities to accomplish the results we want to see in our ministries and the lives of the youth we work with."[7]

This sounded much more like what I was experiencing. Those times I would get caught up in programming, I usually missed what God was doing. At the worst of times, I made my priority more on the program than a young person. It killed relationships and put a chasm between me and my values.

Years later, Andrew Root's *Revisiting Relational Youth Ministry* filled in more gaps of the performance myth. In this book, he echoes what I was convinced of already. When I focus on my own outcomes, relationships suffer.

> *Ministry, then, is not about "using" relationships to get individuals to accept a "third thing," whether that be conservative politics, moral behaviors or even the gospel message. Rather, ministry is about connection, one to another, about sharing in suffering and joy, about persons meeting persons with no pretense or secret motives. It is about shared life, confessing Christ not outside the relationship but within it. This, I learned, was living the gospel.*
>
> —Andrew Root[8]

I began to see youth ministry as something different. Instead of spending most of my time trying to manufacture a short list of outcomes, I committed myself to a process.

Process

As I began to understand my role as a youth worker, new methods of ministry formed. If what Mike King and Andrew Root wrote is true, then I had to find a new way. I couldn't just rely on being a funny, fun-loving leader. Excellent PowerPoint presentations, fog machines, worship, speaking, and even Bible studies are all great, but they can't be the focus. I was reminded of a veteran youth minister who told me, "Programs happen when practices don't." *Ouch!*

Relationships had to move beyond small-group times and Bible studies. They had to form without agendas. My own ideas about what a young person should do needed to take a back seat to what God was already doing in his or her life. Instead of just preparing a lesson, I needed to listen intently to the Holy Spirit. In each person I met with, I had to spend more energy listening, watching, and praying than in remembering my teaching points.

Eventually, I began to see my watering and planting as discipleship like Jesus did so many years ago. I consumed the Gospels, looking for the Jesus way of doing ministry. John 5 became a rallying point for most of what I would do.

One day in Jesus' ministry, he healed a lame man. Most people reflecting on that day would focus on the miraculous event and praise God for his love and compassion. Not the Jewish leaders. Instead they couldn't get past the fact that Jesus did this amazing work on the Sabbath. So they confronted Jesus about working on the Sabbath.

If I were Jesus, I probably would have just pointed to the lame guy walking and shrugged. But Jesus tries to help them see a simple work of faith.

So Jesus explained, "I tell you the truth, the Son can do nothing by himself. He does only what he sees the Father doing. Whatever the Father does, the Son also does. For the Father loves the Son and shows him everything he is doing. In fact, the Father will show him how to do even greater works than healing this man. Then you will truly be astonished. For just as the Father gives life to those he raises from the dead, so the Son gives life to anyone he wants. In addition, the Father judges no one. Instead, he has given the Son absolute authority to judge, so that everyone will honor the Son, just as they honor the Father. Anyone who does not honor the Son is certainly not honoring the Father who sent him.

John 5:19-23, NLT

In this short explanation, Jesus taught me the value of participation. Instead of bringing my own outcomes into the lives of young adults, I need to watch for God's work and join in.

Here lies the value of process ministry. It frees us from having to perform because the true results are so far beyond our abilities.

A process mindset thrives on God-centered participation instead of self-centered results. Because God directs the results, it allows us to commit to being faithful to him and his plans. It also helps the discipleship process to become personal.

How It Works

Planning someone's life, what they should do or look like or act like, is impossible without knowing them intimately—and knowing the future. We just can't accurately do anything more than guess at what a person's life should look like. With this understanding, why would we try?

Process discipleship hinges on a very basic theology found in Ephesians 2:10. If we are God's workmanship, created in Christ to do good works, then everything we need is already inside us because of our relationship to Christ. I'm not saying we have everything we need on our own, but that God has created us intentionally in his image with the ability to do amazing works through our relationship with him.

Presencing

When we change our emphasis from trying to manufacture outcomes, it frees us to be present when we meet with teenagers. Instead of having a prepared message, we can be responsive to their needs and the Holy Spirit's direction.

Early on in my ministry training I took a class with Dr. Richard Pratt. I remember being nervous about what would be expected of me. Dr. Pratt began the class explaining the curriculum and readings, but then, in his typical fashion, threw the syllabus aside and said something that captured everyone's attention.

"All of these assignments you will work alone. In this class, we will work on your presuppositions. My job is to protect the church, from you."

The bomb dropped, and a gasp actually escaped from some students' mouths. That beautiful, challenging moment will live in my memory forever. I realized then that I brought a lot into my relationships. As I lived in the tension of this new reality for me, I began to see how I superimposed myself in places I shouldn't.

When I drive, my ego rides shotgun. So if someone

should cut me off, I am appreciably offended. On a really bad day, I might even wave in an ungracious way to vent my indignation. Inside, I scream, "How dare someone treat me this way? They did that on purpose just to infuriate me!" Really, it has nothing to do with me. Maybe their dog threw up on their way out the door, or their daughter spilt chocolate milk on their shirt, causing them to be late. It really has nothing to do with me.

Searching for outcomes puts me into a certain mindset. It looks for causes, sometimes irrationally. I make situations about me that aren't about me, and those that are about me, I blame on others. When I have disagreements, I can easily find another person's faults while ignoring my own. All so I can reach a self-righteous outcome.

Presencing takes my pursuit of outcomes away and replaces them with value and purpose. Instead of reacting to life from a fixed perspective, I can change with a fluidity based on who I am in relation to the world. This sounds really philosophical, but it's actually very practical.

In every ministry I have served in, I have taught the basics of the faith. Who is Jesus? The Son of God, Savior, Lord, friend, priest, and brother only scratch the surface, right? I teach these truths so young Christians know who God is.

In presencing, I still teach these same basics, but I can go beyond the facts. Because Jesus is your Savior, what does that mean about you? As an individual who is uniquely created to do live an epic life, what should your response be to a Savior who also calls you his friend? These questions push into a personal realm of a person because there isn't one specific answer. Maybe in response they would say they pray more or read the Bible more, but the individual responds out of their heart for a friend.

Instead of the rote ways of living a "Christian" life, they will dig into their personality for what means the most to them and share it. In the years I have asked these kinds of questions, I have heard, if Jesus is my friend and Lord:

"I need to remember that when I'm dancing, because it's when I feel closest to God."

"It's like being friends with Bill Gates, only Jesus doesn't have to wear glasses. I can ask for a lot more in my friendship."

"Sometimes I treat God like a vending machine. I want to just hang out more."

The point is, when we free ourselves from a formulaic approach to youth ministry with a narrow list of possible outcomes, we can see so much more of what God is doing.

Revealing

I have a problem with spiritual formation. Maybe it's just the words themselves, because I have received a lot from my experiences in formation. It's similar to the W.W.J.D. problem. In formation, the goal is to be formed into the likeness of Jesus. It seems like a great goal, but it can also be incredibly misleading.

Jesus is the God-man. He holds the tension of being human and God at the same time. I can't begin the plumb the depths of this mystery. In fact, there are just too many ways I'm not like Christ to make it a simple goal in my life (or one of my youth's life).

Instead of trying get them to be just like Jesus, I spend more time trying to reveal a teen's created identity in Christ. Again, Ephesians 2:10 tells me we are God's workmanship created in Christ for good works. So I commit to the process of bringing that part of a person to life. It's more spiritually revealing than spiritual formation.

When I focus more on uncovering the person God created instead of trying to get them to have certain characteristics, then I don't push for outcomes. As a young person's unique identity is seen, surprising results happen.

My first experience with this was with a pastor's son who was in my youth group at the time. He was very close to graduation and had not yet shown any interest in college. His father was gently nudging here and there to help his son take some initiative, but the son wasn't responding in the way he wanted. In our group time, the son vented his frustration with his dad's pressure to find a school. It was a set outcome.

As intently as I could, I asked him what he wanted to do when he graduated. He mumbled that he wasn't sure. He could recite scripture from memory, talk about grace in an informed way, and probably could even explain *dispensationalism*, but he had no idea what he wanted to do. Like pre-prom girls who haven't been asked out, his created self was still lurking in the shadows just waiting to be asked out.

It would have been easy to stop there and resume my lesson plan, but something felt wrong about that path. I pressed, asking him more and more about his favorite activities and interests. Finally after a progressively honest interrogation, he admitted his deepest desire. He wanted to be in theater and one day be a producer or director. Okay! Now I had something to work with.

From that one honest confession began a young man's direction in life. He went home that night and told his father he wanted to visit some colleges and look at their drama programs.

I was equally humbled and baffled. Here was a guy I had met with for over a year and never knew what he loved doing. When I concerned myself only with an outcomes approach, all I got was a meager commitment to those outcomes. Giving up on that to pursue a person's passions surprised me. God was doing way more than I could have imagined. The Lord revealed in a single moment a teenager's unique purpose for his life. In the years following, that moment found depth as this young man grew in his talent. It didn't end that night. I think it might continue to be revealed his whole life.

Ends and Means

> *"It is far easier to decide on a desired end, a goal, than it is to acquire the adequate means."*
>
> —Eugene Peterson[9]

While I have made a case for changing the priority in discipleship from outcomes-based to process, outcomes still carry weight. Very few adolescents will try something new without seeing results. The bigger change here rests in discernment. Change happens daily in our lives. In teenagers, whose lives consist of dramatic changes in short amounts of time, it becomes a microcosm. Because so much is completely new to them, they can try on new identities quickly and easy. One week they may be moody and disengaged wearing only black. The next they may be winsome and flowery. So change is always happening. The work in process discipleship is to point out these changes so benefits can be seen.

Since reaching a certain age, I have had to change my way of eating. My wife used to chide me about regularly eating ice cream at 10:00 P.M. It never seemed to have any negative effect, though; at least not until I got a little time (and girth) under my belt. I probably did make some kind of vow to myself as a child that, when I grew up, I would eat whatever I liked. The years have proved this to be an unwise choice.

As my eating changed, so did my health. But I didn't notice any change without a little help. After cutting soda out of my diet, my wife asked me one day how I felt. I knew I felt better, but it wasn't until that moment I connected it with a difference in my nutrition.

Working with teens mirrors a similar realization. They need to see the effects of their choices. They want to. My role in working with them hinges on helping them see God's work in their lives and to see how it benefits them. Even if a choice takes a while to have results, they need to see something to affirm their efforts. In later chapters, I will address this in full, but for now, remember that the biggest rewards and changes happen internally. Feelings can be a much bigger payoff than behaviors.

Case Study

Evelyn was a lively girl with a cherubic face. She loved performing with the high school band and was constantly surrounded by her close group of nine friends. Making the grade and getting along at home were never a problem for her. It seemed as if she had an ideal life; but she had a dark secret.

Early in her childhood, Evelyn was sexually molested by a family member. It happened regularly over a period of years without anyone else in the family knowing. When her parents found out, they wanted to protect her from her abuser. They decided the best thing to do was to not tell anyone and move on. They would keep an eye on the family member who had abused her, but they wouldn't change anything else.

As Evelyn grew into a beautiful young woman, she began to realize the effect of her emotional trauma. The pet name her father called her began to feel derisive. It reminded her of her mistreatment. Other little things began to provoke a severe response in her. So late in her high school career, Evelyn started counseling with a great therapist.

Through the help of her counselor, she began to see why she responded to people differently because of her sexual assault. Connections were made in her relationships with her family and friends, revealing the damage done by her family member. She felt she was ready to move on, and her therapist agreed; so she ended her treatment.

Later, she told me her story. It was a sacred moment for her to confess all that had happened to her. Likely, she felt empowered in being able to tell the story. But something still wasn't right. She said she would sometimes be filled with rage when remembering her past. Other times she would get depressed at seemingly random times. Through tears of anguish she told me all she wanted was to make it go away. She had forgiven her abuser, but the feelings wouldn't leave.

Evelyn was committed to the outcome of moving past her molestation. She desperately wanted to forgive and forget. Unfortunately, forgiveness isn't always an outcome we can reach. For deep pains in our lives, it's often more like a process. Evelyn was frustrated with herself because she held her goal of forgiveness as a one-time event. It limited her ability to deal with her feelings of being a victim.

I suggested after our meeting that she change her goal for herself.

Maybe it would be a better goal to know what to do with her feelings when they came than to beat herself up for having them. We worked on ways for her to acknowledge her feelings when they came. I reminded her as often as I could that forgiveness is a process. Every time she had these feelings, they were never wrong. Each time she would relive a part of her pain and needed to forgive again.

I don't know for certain, but I think eventually the feelings did go away. I'm certain they diminished. What I do know is this: the ability to look beyond a set of outcomes frees us from a dead end. It gives us the ability to look beyond the present and do something leading to health. Committing to the process is often much more important than striving for certain outcomes.

Chapter 3
Dynamic over Static

"I never liked jazz music because jazz music doesn't resolve. But I was outside the Bagdad Theater in Portland one night when I saw a man playing the saxophone. I stood there for fifteen minutes, and he never opened his eyes.
After that I liked jazz music.
Sometimes you have to watch somebody love something before you can love it yourself. It is as if they are showing you the way.
I used to not like God because God didn't resolve. But that was before any of this happened."

—Donald Miller[10]

The Fruit Factory

I was never a frugivorous person. Maybe the blame falls on my family who rarely had fruit in the house, or I might have just been born like this. Either way, the taste of fruit never appealed to me.

At times I felt lonely in my aversion. Friends seemed to enjoy a pulpy snack so thoroughly that I felt like an outcast among foodies. I remember one late spring soccer game where orange slices were passed out to the players as an energy boost. Casually pocketing my slice, I pretended to enjoy it so I wouldn't feel the shame of my evasion of citrus. At another time I confessed my distaste to my wife. That marital rift may never heal. I assumed that pulpy seed-bearing plants would never be pleasing to my palate.

One day, though, after watching a particularly convicting documentary, my wife started going to the local farmers' market. She returned with randomly sized baskets of seasonal goodies, changing my presumption of the sweet fleshy produce and its taste. Guilt played a part, I have to admit, in my new open-mindedness toward trying this new food staple. I began with something easy—strawberries. Of all the fruit I didn't like, these little red buds I disliked the least.

To my surprise I actually enjoyed them. They weren't like the fruit I had previously experienced. These berries labeled *straw* tasted nothing like it. Whoever named strawberries has obviously never tasted fresh produce from the farmers' market. These were red through and through with tiny hairs poking the roof of my mouth. Bursting with flavor, they tasted like strawberries cubed. I realized something that first day of deliverance from an aversion to fruit—supermarket produce doesn't compare to fresh, seasonal fruit.

This realization built for me an analogy I have come to rely on in the church. Just as "super" market fruit doesn't compare to fresh, local fruit, the attractional church of set outcomes doesn't compare to the organic church free from presuppositions. Yeah, that's a loaded statement if I've ever seen one. Don't get me wrong, there are many large churches with a wonderful, time-proven legacy of faith, but the word "mega" seems to do to the church what "super" does to the market. In the path to becoming bigger, many churches lose something essential in the faith of believers. This is equally true of attractional youth ministries that care more about presentation and getting people in the door than substance.

One author and statistician described the state of the church similarly:

We are at a critical point in the life of the North American church; the Christian community must rethink our efforts to make disciples.

Many of the assumptions on which we have built our work with young people are rooted in modern, mechanistic, and mass production paradigms. Some (though not all) ministries have taken cues from the assembly line, doing everything possible to streamline the manufacture of shiny new Jesus-followers, fresh from the factory floor. But disciples cannot be mass-produced. Disciples are handmade, one relationship at a time.

—David Kinnaman[11]

The church and especially its youth ministries have spent a lot of time and effort trying to appear healthy. I'm not saying it has been an intentional cover-up, but the focus on looks instead of substance is evident. Just surf the web to almost any church website. Pictures of happy, smiling people will adorn its webpages. There will usually be a statement of faith and a page dedicated to the leaders. Each of the ministries will get a page too, showing more self-contented people maybe during worship, intently listening to a sermon, or youth standing next to a recently painted building wielding paintbrushes. I dare you to find a church website with a person crying on the front page, or someone struggling with addiction. I tripledog-dare you.

These kinds of stories, where the ruins of teenagers' lives are put back together, don't make the front page. They should. The church should be known as the place of redemption and healing. It should reflect the work Jesus did so many years ago when he was physically present among us. Truthfully, a lot of these churches probably have moments like this, but they hide among the hurt and lonely. Instead of a culture that celebrates God's work, we often sing the latest worship song. How will the church become what Isaiah described as a holy people, redeemed and sought after?

After asking many church leaders about the absence of these crucial elements of the church, I got a mixed bag of answers. Mostly, it came down to the idea that visitors don't like them. It might scare people to know a former prostitute is among them or that someone struggling with an alternative lifestyle sits in the pew next to them. The church doesn't want to be known for that. Instead it turns a person's struggle into a nice safe phrase like "alternative lifestyle."

So, like the fruit factories, appearance takes precedence over substance. It prefers ripe-looking fruit to nutritious, tastebud-bursting flavor. That's what happens with a formulaic model for church. We can't blame the church altogether though. Our culture supports this flawed idea. Aren't our schools working from a similar model?

Sir Ken Robinson summarized it when he said,

The fact is that given the challenges we face, education doesn't need to be reformed—it needs to be transformed. The key to this transformation is not to standardize education, but to personalize it, to build achievement on discovering the individual talents of each child, to put students in an environment where they want to learn and where they can naturally discover their true passions.
—Ken Robinson[12]

For discipleship to become effective again, we have a lot to unlearn. It will mean turning from our cultural assumptions and embracing a different understanding of growth and even success.

The Checklist

I remember my early childhood in the church. Every Sunday my parents would cajole me into rising early enough to get ready. Because I came from a frugal (cheap) family, I would then don the itchiest polyester pants imaginable. They almost covered my ankles, but at least I was prepared for a flood should God's wrath come once again. A white button-down oxford with black dress shoes and socks completed the ensemble. I wasn't much for accessorizing.

My older brother and sister and I would all pile into our white '69 Buick station wagon and make the trip to church. Millbrook Baptist Church was a typical place of worship in the south. People would trudge into their respective Sunday school classes. We would each receive an envelope with a checklist on the back. Read Bible daily, check. Prayed daily, check. Shared the gospel, check. I didn't know anybody who actually did these things, so I just checked off my list and put in my two quarters, given to me by my parents, and sealed the envelope tight.

It wasn't until I was an early teen that I started wondering about this checklist. Did other teenagers in my youth group actually do all of that stuff? Lying about it seemed like the best way to handle it, but the Bible and the pastor said we shouldn't lie. I was confounded. I had no idea what sharing the gospel even meant. My red, faux-leather King James Version Bible seemed equally stupefying.

Faced with feelings of betrayal for my hypocritical checkmarks, I did what a lot of teenagers probably do.

I concluded the church had a very weird system of life that I couldn't relate to. If these were the checklists safeguarding me from hell, I guess I was doomed.

Beyond Checklists

Much later in life when I became a youth pastor, I knew these checklists, though still prevalent, weren't something I missed. And while I didn't hand out envelopes as youth walked in the door, I began to realize the churches I served had their own checklists. In the south, we would say, "Don't drink, don't smoke, don't chew, and don't hang out with girls that do." I never knew a girl who chewed tobacco, but I'm absolutely sure I wouldn't be tempted to date her if we met.

What can I say? I grew up in Alabama.

As I moved to different areas of the country, though, I saw the common qualities youth ministries were supposed to have. Adolescents should stay out of trouble. That means no partying, pregnancies, or suspensions from school. They should get good grades and dress appropriately. Questioning parents or teachers was looked down on, though not forbidden. Swearing was also on the naughty list.

While these rules were common wherever I served, they were confused by cultural qualifiers. Swearing was wrong, unless you were the star basketball player for the church team. Then an occasional lapse was understandable. Teens shouldn't drink, but going to a questionable party where alcohol was surely present was tolerable, especially if the teenager needed to make some friends. It all became confusing until I met Jeff and Steve.

Six months into my time with a church, I was approached by two sets of parents. They both had sons who were best friends since childhood. Neither of them went to their "home"church. The parentals wanted me to connect with their sons in hopes that they would come back to their family's church. It still baffles me that the parents didn't just tell them to come with them, but that's a story for another time.

So, under pressure from their parents, I met with the two friends at the only viable breakfast restaurant available in Butler, Pennsylvania, known as Eat'n Park. Both of them were actively involved in a church similar to their parents' church, where most of their friends attended. I knew the youth pastor at that church and couldn't find anything wrong with it.

Through breakfast I asked each of them about school and what they liked to do after school. They were both seniors, so I got their plans for post graduation. They were polite, and conversation was easy for them. It wasn't long before they needed to leave to make it to school on time. As our time drew to an end, Jeff asked me what I wanted to talk to them about. Jeff's hands had suddenly tied themselves in knots, and he was desperately trying to stare them open. He knew his parents had put me up to something. It took a while, but I finally assured him that I agreed to meet with them and didn't have any other motives.

I think Jeff, who operated as the spokesman for the duo, was so shocked he offered to meet again. So the next Thursday morning, we were in the same booth sharing stories and scrambled eggs. As the time came to leave, Jeff asked me again, "Wasn't there something you wanted to tell us?" I told him I had fulfilled my promise to their parents to meet with them. The look of surprise on his face was unforgettable. When he asked if we could meet again, I just smiled.

From that moment on, we met every Thursday morning until they graduated. I realized something significant had happened. Because I didn't have an agenda, they wanted to continue meeting together.

Through that time together, Jeff would regularly ask me what I thought about his life. He was fishing for my checklist. I never took the bait, but instead asked him to make his own checklist. It wasn't long before they both started telling me about their struggles and asking for help. Through that time with Jeff and Steve, I learned the value of a dynamic relationship

I could have come in every Thursday with a lesson or an idea, making me look more impressive to them. It would probably even have won over their trust and established me as an authority in their lives. But for some reason, I trusted the direction God was taking during our time together. I was able to suspend my formula for "contact work" and respond to each of these guys as they shared their lives with me.

What I found out in this time was that the Holy Spirit could be trusted. God himself would direct conversation around what he was doing in the people I meet with. In fact, my relationship with Jeff and Steve continues even after a decade of geographic separation. All evidence points to this being a better way than my efforts to systematically disciple someone with my own method for success.

How It Works

As I wrote in chapter 2, outcomes can mislead discipleship. It can set false goals for teenagers you are discipling. Similarly, formulas can be just as misleading. They insist on following one path to reach a specific goal, instead of allowing God to lead the trail. Being a dynamic instead of static discipler hinges on several basic ideas.

- *God wants to grow the people I meet with (even more than I do).*
- *He knows more than I do.*
- *Not every person needs to have the same goals.*
- *There are many ways to get to the same place.*

Being dynamic rests mostly in your ability to know yourself and to embrace your limitations. When you see it as your responsibility to change people for the better, all you can hope to do is react to others. Reacting is a selfish pursuit in relationships because it follows your own agenda. Responding is the dynamic way to disciple.

Suppose I meet with a student who is struggling with cutting, and I also have a history of cutting. I can be a great resource for someone, or I can superimpose my path onto theirs, forcing them into only one direction. If I react to them, I can't separate their problems from my own. My solutions have to be their solutions because they worked for me. Reacting is insistent.

If, however, I can be open to more than one outcome for God's plan in their recovery, then I can respond to them directly. This allows for many possible ways to see God's direction and guidance. I can only do this when I separate my own path from theirs. The failure to separate myself from the other in counseling is called transference. It's a very real weakness for those who empathize easily with others. What's needed is discernment.

I constantly remember Ephesians 2:10 in my discipleship relationships. Each person I meet with is God's masterpiece, created in Christ for good works. Relating to someone dynamically sends me to Ephesians 1:18 where

Paul writes, "I pray that the eyes of your heart may be enlightened in order that you may know the hope to which he has called you, the riches of his glorious inheritance in his holy people" (NIV).

Discipleship offers hope. It builds a place of trust in young people, telling them they can do great things because they were created to be great. The most effective tool in dynamic discipleship is in pointing out what God is already doing.

If I respond to my student who has the cutting issue by giving her directions to follow, her value rests in her ability to carry out those directions. It might turn out OK for her, but it might also send her further into her problem. If instead I can respond to what I see God already doing, then I can allow the freedom for God to direct her.

To do this, I can acknowledge her pain, her willingness to talk to me about it, and her trust to hope for something better. With confident assurance, I can definitely offer her hope.

From a personal perspective, I wondered why my faith wasn't as splendid. Was there something to the spiritual disciplines of reading my Bible daily, praying daily, witnessing to the lost that left my spirit wanting? Maybe. I remember early on giving to the Baptist missionary Lottie Moon offering and thinking, "Who was this Lottie, and what is she doing now?"

Crossing off a checklist of actions didn't seem to produce in me the kind of resplendence I longed for. I always felt as if I were lagging behind everyone else. Somehow, I thought I didn't measure up to the people around me. This life I was teaching teens to grasp felt like a set of laws that I couldn't keep myself.

Case Study

I met Glenn through a missionary dating effort of one the girls in my youth group. He was a good-looking guy. As he got more serious with his girlfriend, he started coming to our meetings. Glenn was a questioner. I loved having him in our gatherings because he would always ask great questions.

As I got to know him, I started meeting together with Glenn for breakfast once a week. Glenn was a serious student of the Bible (he later became a pastor). As much as I would try to prepare some new bit of theology for him, I would always get sidetracked with one of his queries. It wasn't long until I gave up preparing special insights for him and began relying on his prompts to direct our time together.

This all came to a head when Glenn asked me, "Paul, how far is too far in a dating relationship?" He was staring at me with so much intensity it would have bored a hole into a normal human, but not a youth worker.

"If you're asking me that question, it's too far," I told him. I really wanted it to be the end of the conversation, but Glenn was unflappable. For the rest of the morning he grilled me on the appropriateness of affection for a dating teen. None of my pat answers would stop his incessant probing for answers.

I realized through my meetings with young adults that I had shifted my priority. Instead of planning these times together, banking on my ability to bring fresh teaching to them, I began to listen more. As my listening sharpened, I was able to respond to their needs and help them infinitely more than my planning allowed. It seems obvious when I say it like this, but my relationships needed to be dynamic.

Responding to people overrode my ability to prepare a
lesson for them.

Chapter 4
Heuristic over Algorithmic

"Begin with complexity. Behavioral scientists often divide what we do on the job or learn in school into two categories: "algorithmic" and "heuristic." An algorithmic task is one in which you follow a set of established instructions down a single pathway to one conclusion. That is, there's an algorithm for solving it. A heuristic task is the opposite. Precisely because no algorithm exists for it, you have to experiment with possibilities and devise a novel solution."

—Daniel H. Pink[13]

Learning to "Like" Tomatoes

"Tomatoes are disgusting!" Those words came from a friend in college whom I will call Karen to protect her dignity. My memory of that time and her exact words may be compromised, but I definitely remember the sentiment. She did NOT like raw tomatoes. Both the flavor and the texture had her gagging. Karen wasn't someone I would call a picky eater, so this one emphatic dislike was memorable.

Her distaste for tomatoes made for an interesting scene months after she made this declaration, when Karen's romantic life took a twist in the form of a different love interest. The new guy wasn't a part of our normal group of friends, so he didn't know of Karen's prejudice against the "love apple." He was a bit divergent from the regulars in our cluster of friends. Today, most people would call him a hippie or health nut, but when I was in college, we called people like him "crunchy" or "granola."

Months after hearing Karen's passionate distaste for tomatoes, I saw her eating lunch in the cafeteria with her new male acquaintance. Want to guess what she was eating? That's right, tomatoes! Clueless of the happenings of love and the compromises of the heart, I confronted Karen's obvious lack of conviction, saying, "Hey, Karen, I thought you didn't like tomatoes." Mr. Crunchy's face was incredulous, and Karen's expression clearly told me I'd made a mistake. I quickly retreated but still wasn't convinced of her newfound love for tomatoes.

I decided to stick around for a while. Picking up some lunch, I positioned myself within easy view of Karen. From the corner of my eye, I noticed every time she ate a tomato, she made a face. It wasn't the ecstatic face of someone eating chocolate, either. This was the face of someone who had just opened a gym bag full of sweaty clothes left by a thirteen-year-old boy after a junior high lock-in. Aha! The face confirmed it. She really didn't like tomatoes! Why would she be eating them if she didn't like them?

It took me a while to figure it out, but I eventually understood. You've probably already come to your own conclusion as well. She liked the guy she was dating enough to try something she thought she didn't like. You might say her desire for him overcame her dislike of tomatoes. She eventually learned to like tomatoes through that experience, though it was well after Mr. Crunchy had come and gone.

I learned something important about motivations through that experience.

1. We can't change what we like.
2. What we like can change.
3. People in love are crazy.

Behave

This realization with Karen changed the way I disciple young adults. Karen couldn't be told she had to like something to be accepted. That would have seemed oppressive. She had to decide on her own if it was worth it. Even then, she couldn't change what she liked (or disliked). It was only after trying tomatoes for a while that she overcame her distaste. This is often the case with discipling youth as well.

Within every young person, there is an immediate resistance when told they have to do anything. I don't blame them. Who likes being told they have to do something? Here lies a problem with so many young adults. Many of them are formed and influenced by parents who mostly want a wholesome alternative space for their children. They want an activity to keep them busy and out of trouble. This idea solidifies in school, where behaviorism is the number one sifting tool for classes.

The church made friends with this motive long ago, when it reduced faith into a moral code. This idea crept into the church through countless Bible studies and book club meetings. The equation is clear, if the problem is behavior, the remedy is education. Most of the church's time and energy is spent teaching. I once heard a pastor say, "Right thinking leads to right living." With all of the moral failures in the church, that doesn't seem likely. If right thinking would solve our problems, they would be gone by now wouldn't they?

So the agenda of many youth ministries in these churches becomes a moral one. Teenagers hear a consistent message focusing on behavior they don't get to choose. It shouldn't surprise anyone that this generation of young people takes little ownership in religion. They're highly spiritual but lack a direction for acting on their faith.

Through this perspective, the church reduced discipleship to education with an agenda. That agenda, behavior, is the tomato of the church. To fit in and be accepted, you have to eat the church's red savory fruit. This idea doesn't make much sense, though, when you look at Jesus' ministry. Where the church is known for being judgmental and hypocritical, he was known for being welcoming and accepting. Jesus recruited his disciples knowing they wouldn't act like other religious leaders. That obviously wasn't the point for Jesus' way of growing disciples.

Discipleship and Autonomy

Much like Karen, Jesus' disciples exercised lots of freedom. They understood more and more about liberty as they spent time with Jesus. How many times did he have to defend something the apostles did? The Bible tells story after story, from ceremonial washing to eating on the Sabbath, showing that those following Jesus broke rules others took very seriously. Jesus' way of discipleship made a necessity of personal latitude in his followers.

Discipleship thrives in the freedom of an autonomous relationship. I'm not saying young adults don't need clear direction. But I'm sure they also need the freedom to explore new ideas in their own way. For this reason, discipleship can't rely on a preset system of likes and dislikes. It can't describe every situation, decide the best outcome, and then list a series of steps to get there. It can't be a formula. Behavior shouldn't be the single goal of discipleship. That mentality fails the person God created as an individual because it denies the significance of each teenager we see.

A Different Goal

When God created us, it was in his image. At the same time, we thrive in our own uniqueness. It's obvious in how we personalize our lives. Mobile phones dominate our culture. Walking through any mall, you are bound to come across a kiosk of phone covers and cases. How many different versions of the same cover are really needed? One company actually makes personalized cases from your own artwork. The point is, we love expressing ourselves and flourish in being unique. Hindering that creative spirit butts against the freedom of humanity. It contradicts the very essence of God's design for humankind.

Because young adults need liberation, making them behave fails. Behaviorism doesn't allow for the self-direction of the individual. Instead it ends with a lot of faked morals. If, instead, the goal of discipleship is to help teens realize their identity in Christ, then it should be concerned with motivation. That independence should move young adults to act on their faith and not consistently rely on the voice of culture.

The Apostle Paul describes this freedom in his letter to the church in Rome saying, "Don't copy the behavior and customs of this world, but let God transform you into a new person by changing the way you think" (Romans 12:2a, NLT).

It's clear that God is the one who transforms young people, and he does it internally. Dictating a predetermined response for a teenager doesn't reflect this thought. In fact, it falls more closely into the "behavior and custom" of the world. This way of discipleship at best only causes shame. In the worst mode, it promotes dishonesty when teens realize they can't ever fully measure up to any list of rights and wrongs.

Studying the life of the apostle Paul, it's easy to identify some key traits he possessed allowing him to be the apostle to the churches in Asia. Paul wrapped his theology around reason. It was an essential part of his identity. It helped him meander through disagreements in the many churches he served. Discipleship can't take this one trait, reason, and make it the goal for every follower of Christ. This type of program asks that all Christians have the same traits as Paul to be effective in ministry. It doesn't allow for differing contexts or individuality. Even worse, it doesn't give any freedom for a person to find her own God-given gifts that will make her what God intended.

About Freedom

Desire is a funny thing. It can be just as demotivating as it is motivating. What if you told a teenager he should become a janitor, specifically that he has a knack for cleaning toilets? After cringing about what that implies about him, he'd probably question your judgment. If, however, he came to that thought on his own, he might accept that career because of his freedom to choose. As much of stretch as this seems, there are motivators that would make a teen want to become a janitor.

On one of my many summer mission trips, there was a 12-year-old boy who wanted nothing more than to clean up after all of our work.

During the day, he shuffled around from one project to another looking for something he could do. Weighing maybe 100 pounds soaking wet, he wasn't able to do much of the work some of the older teenagers were doing. So I asked him what he would like to do. He chose to clean up. In the choice to pick a suitable task, he felt like he was an effective part of the team. Cleaning our worksite didn't inspire "oohs" and "ahs" from our team, but it did garner lots of "thank yous" from some of our older leaders. That feeling of satisfaction he felt at the end of every day knowing he did his part was more motivating than his feeling of being helpless.

In his book *Drive*, Daniel Pink describes what discipleship has known for centuries. External motivators like salary and prizes only motivate in the short term. In the long term, they actually demotivate and limit performance.

> *Meanwhile, instead of restraining negative behavior, rewards and punishments can often set it lose—and give rise to cheating, addiction and dangerous myopic thinking. This is weird. And it doesn't hold in all circumstances... many practices whose effectiveness we take for granted produce counterintuitive results: they give us less of what we want—and more of what we don't want.*
> —Daniel H. Pink[14]

Pink cites a study discerning autonomy as one of the three basic needs of human beings. You could argue the point of the three basic needs, but there's something important in all of us that confirms our need for freedom. The Bible supports this idea.

"Now, the Lord is the Spirit, and wherever the Spirit

of the Lord is, there is freedom" (2 Corinthians 3:17, NLT).

"Why should my freedom be limited by what someone else thinks?" (1 Corinthians 10:29b, NLT).

Apparently, God wants us to be free, but it's easy for our desires and their realization to trap us. If a 15-year-old girl thinks the only way to fit in is to wear a certain type of clothes, then she accepts the snare of acceptance. She is forced to choose: either dress however she likes and risk losing her peers, or let others choose her wardrobe and gain their acknowledgement. This decision feels like it takes away her choice because she deeply wants acceptance. Like Karen, it's a subtle, but self-enforced decision between supposed acceptance and freedom. The sad truth is this decision rarely gets tested daily in the lives of adolescents.

Our desires can go awry here. Given enough rope, teens hang themselves on the hope of measuring up. Since there's so much pressure to fit in, and very little pressure to be themselves, they cave to the need to belong. Few of them have the courage to be themselves and see if they will be accepted on their own terms.

This is far from a black-and-white decision where they only do one thing or the other, though. Teens rarely lose themselves completely. Instead, freedom gives way little by little until a veneer forms over them. This facade obscures the real person inside and shapes the very behaviors the church has tried to correct. If they are unable to make this choice, faith in their created identity isn't realized. The opportunity for them to see their trust in God fails as well. They don't see the opportunity for Jesus to reveal himself through their relationships. Freedom is removed from their context simply because they won't take the chance.

Safety in Freedom

"For you have been called to live in freedom, my brothers and sisters. But don't use your freedom to satisfy your sinful nature. Instead, use your freedom to serve one another in love." Galatians 5:13, NLT

What this scripture points to is the proper and improper use of freedom. The sinful nature needs to be affirmed and stroked to continue having power over a person. But serving in love, as the Bible tells us, is a selfless place of honesty allowing us the freedom to be accepted for our true self, instead of the safety of our image. No wonder we get caught up in trying to impress others with the coolest cell phone cases. This false freedom is safe simply because it has no bearing on who we really are.

It's easy to see how we use the safety of what we like, instead of the deeper desires defining us. When we are criticized for our preferences, we have a way of dismissing that criticism. We can easily abandon it for another like. We can just give up on one thing we like and move on to another.

At the very same time, we feel the need to commit to one thing. We want to be known through that thing. In the cavernous blood pump inside us, we know there is something consistently stable in our lives. We can't change our likes all of the time just because of other people's criticism without feeling like a fraud. It's the freedom to choose our likes that is essential if we are going to motivated to change. This is the essential nature of autonomy.

Looking at Karen, it's easy to decipher this paradox. If her boyfriend told her she had to like tomatoes to go out with him, then she almost certainly wouldn't have. The demand would have killed her desire for getting to know him. On the other hand, the freedom for her to try tomatoes and learn to like them allowed her desire for companionship to thrive.

The False God

Autonomy and motivation in discipleship are necessary for one more reason, though there are many. Often leaders become the focus of discipleship. If this happens, then they become god instead of relying God's Spirit to lead. How tempting it is for a leader to become so important to another. It's the savory sweetness of effectiveness and power. If a disciple relies completely on the leader, then the disciple is handicapped by that need.

Giving young disciples autonomy becomes essential for them as they learn to hear God's voice for themselves. A mentor can't always be there to tell them what God is saying; and at some point in the future, they will graduate.

Created Identity

If discipleship has a goal, it's to help youth realize a deep sense of identity (self). It should nurture a place of trust in a person's identity that overrules outside pressures. There isn't anything wrong with a friendship between teens based on their favorite music or preference for Hello Kitty cell phone covers, but it can't be the foundation of an individual. I am convinced there is only one way to discover a person's true self. It comes from knowing Jesus. If you've been in church, it probably doesn't sound new to you, but let me unpack this a bit.

In his letter to the church in Ephesus, Paul writes, "For we are God's masterpiece. He has created us anew in Christ Jesus, so that we can do the good things he planned for us long ago" (Ephesians 2:10, NLT).

As God's masterpieces, we are created as works of art. Without a perfect relationship, though, our identity becomes obscured. We become formed by our needs and preferences. Most of us chase after things that make our eyes sparkle or our tongues salivate. We are sensual people. When we're not searching for those experiences, we look for those items that help us fit in with the right crowd. At the same time, we want to be recognized as unique and extraordinary. We want to be seen doing great things. Paul tells us through his letter that we are created for "good things." The only way this happens is to be "created anew in Christ."

I'm going to make a point that some people might think is a bit of hairsplitting, but it has become a necessary truth in discipleship for me. There is a difference between our chosen preferences and our deepest desires. What we choose to like is easily seen by looking at our clothes, music, car, house, or whatever describes our appearance. Our deeper desires point to something hidden within us.

Our desires drive all of what is seen in our preferences. Underneath all of our likes lives the deeper sense of our personality. Like our personality, our desires are fairly set and unchanging. Psychologists would say they are formed early in our development, but Paul knew better. He knew our identity was set before the creation of the world and only in knowing our Creator could we know our identity.

Without a sense of identity, people tend to live as slaves to their needs and wants. They constantly feed them as an addiction. The latest fashion, fad, or treasure shapes their behavior and their life. In contrast, discipleship points to the deeper identity in all of us. This causes fear. We spend so much effort trying to hide it. The deeper part of our true selves is sometimes the most feared part of us to reveal to others. We can chase after a healthy self-image, but our identity tells us whether we are truly fulfilled. If we want to live as the new person created in Christ's identity, then we need to take an honest look at our created identity. Only this will show who God created us to be.

We Can't Change What We Like

"Preference is ultimately irrational."
—George Santayana[15]

Ask someone their favorite color and they will tell you—blue, green, magenta. Then ask them why it is their favorite color. They might say, "I like blue because it brings out the color in my eyes." Well, why is that so great? They will probably say they really like the color of their eyes and want people to notice them. Wouldn't a color that creates contrast be just as good? Dig deeper, and you have another preference. Why do they like the color of their eyes? What does that have to do with liking the color blue? The deeper you plunge, the more you realize it just isn't rational. More often, what you find is that one preference points to a deeper desire to be known and loved.

These deeper desires rarely change. For those of us who like to think we are in control of our lives, this is a problem. To make matters worse, our preferences are completely illogical.

I can't waste time in discipleship trying to change a person's likes. This is especially true about morality. If someone has an affinity for scotch and cigars, and the church doesn't allow either, then I will beat my head against the wall trying to change them. I can't expect someone to give up steak just because I have become convinced it's bad for him. Anytime an agenda rules a relationship, I can't expect a change to be anything but fake. Discipling with my own agenda has never produced the results I have wanted. When I've done this, I get frustrated with the disciples' lack of progress, and they end up feeling like they are letting me down all the time. In discipleship, we need to let those expectations go and begin to focus on God's direction. I need to acknowledge my own limitations. I can't change anyone's preferences and will waste time if I make it may goal.

Instead of chasing the winds of preference, I want to acknowledge those deeper desires I see in people and begin diving deeper into how they are moved by them. I want to connect their preferences with the needs they are fulfilling. Realizing those needs, they can then begin to see how the desires of their heart are something God put there. When they start to see that, the real work begins.

What We Like Can Change... IF

When I was young, it was a special treat to wake up on Saturday mornings, because in my house, Saturday mornings meant animated bliss. Every Saturday morning I would wake up early, get a blanket, plop down on our couch and let my imagination run wild. One of my favorite cartoons was Flash Gordon. He was the benchmark for the life I dreamed of. I used to imagine myself having adventures like him. In that world, I would fly across the universe to face unknown dangers, always do the right thing, and always be the hero in that adventure. It was the perfect world for the perfect guy where dreams always came true.

As an adult I recently watched an episode of this thrilling show and was shocked at how awful it was. Plot, story, and animation were all so bad I couldn't finish watching it. Re-experiencing this childhood favorite taught me something about myself and my desires. What I thought was so amazing wasn't anymore. I had changed. My preferences of story, depth, and plot had evolved, and I just couldn't be made to like something as contrived as Flash Gordon again.

When I disciple someone, I notice more of these surface inclinations in the beginning. As I get to know them, I want to begin to see the deeper longing God put there. It takes time and effort to get past the safe image that people are willing to let you see. The most prayerful, discerning heart is required to see through the layers of walls and masks each teenager will present. If I am patient and free of my agendas, I begin to see something. Eventually, the deeper self of that person reveals itself, even if in small bits and pieces. This is when I start to see the true fruit of discipleship.

Now I have to make a decision. I have to decide how to challenge the disciple in his safe preferences and connect it to something deeper. I want to awaken something that has been put to sleep by his own choices of comfort and safety. This is the beginning of tapping the desire to change (motivation). This desire is the need for something better, something larger than life that draws out the deeper desires of the heart. In leading disciples, I want to awaken that longing, which is the beginning of change.

My work then becomes nurturing their desire for change. Their cravings for a different kind of life are what motivate them to change. It's my job in discipling them to see and develop that longing.

The Discipleship Sandbox

When I began to see how the freedom of our deepest desires shapes us as disciples, I realized the roles motivation, desire, and autonomy play in realizing change. Without motivation, the will to change is limited and becomes ineffective. Because of the need for freedom, motivation has to come from within for a person to truly want to change. There has to be that essential autonomy for the desire to change to rise above the need to fit in.

A few years ago there was a phenomenon in the gaming industry known as *Grand Theft Auto*. Whether you were for it or against it because of its content doesn't really matter. What matters is that gamers were rabid for it, and it wasn't because of the graphics or the story. Instead, the gameplay centered around expansive spaces where the player could explore areas and complete missions on his own terms. Like other games, the missions gradually built in difficulty, preparing the player for an eventual showdown. That's what the game designers intended. What actually happened shouldn't have been surprising if you know teenagers. Instead of completing missions, the players starting using the wide-open spaces to play their own games in their own ways. They didn't follow any linear mission progression at all. Instead, they would just drive around trying to get as many police to chase them as possible before dying. Instead of playing by the rules, they would break as many as they could. In hindsight, it has been labeled the sandbox-style gaming, since it resembled the freedom offered to children playing in a sandbox. Sandbox gaming was a revolution in the video game industry that led to other games following the same formula. Gamers finally had freedom and autonomy to play however they wanted, and they ate it up.

Relationships leading to discipleship need to encounter this kind of freedom. Discipleship moves everyday relationships with young adults into a place of freedom and safety pointing to deeper desires. It builds relationships that drive youth forward into previously unrealized character. It challenges their safe lives and moves them toward their real desires, giving them the autonomy to choose where to go next. The challenge to realize how and why they made points to those desires they are discovering that shape and inform their true selves. This is where teens see the first hints of knowing themselves through the eyes of a Creator who calls them his work of art.

The discipleship sandbox uses the same principles as an open sandbox. It gives freedom to students to find their own way and at the same time points to something deeper within them. It points them to a desire that is closer to their created identity. It shows them something about themselves they have always longed for, but have probably not realized. My role in discipleship is to begin to identify those things God has made in a person and open a path of desire to see those things come into play. All the while, I need to recognize my limitations and allow autonomy for the disciple.

Discipleship connects these desires to who God is

and to who they are. This kind of discipleship shows how the desires we have point to something deeper inside us. When a guy looks at a girl and his desire is awakened, it points to something deep inside him that longs for intimacy and closeness. When a girl looks at a fashion magazine and longs to look a certain way, it points to a deeper desire to be thought beautiful by another. These shallow preferences are just the world's twisting of the desires God created us with. They are safe likes that we can hide in for a temporary acceptance of our false selves.

When we can realize our deeper desires and take a first step, we begin to know for ourselves who we really are. Only through realizing our true desires and letting the Spirit of God work in those desires do we become free from the twisting taint of sin in them. Better than all of that, in this freedom to know ourselves, we begin to see the face of God as he reveals his own glory in us. To realize God's glory in us is a staggering thought and is the result of discipleship.

How It Works

All of this might sound really good to you, yet you may not feel close to actually being able to do any of it. How will you see someone's deeper desires that are hidden inside? How will you point to those desires without cutting off autonomy? Here are some methods:

Pray for discernment. Your leadership should always be secondary to the Holy Spirit's. God knows what he created and he knows what will inspire and challenge disciples. Pray and listen for God to show you what he is doing in your disciple.

Watch for what is exciting. Youth will often show

what they are excited about and what motivates them. Just watch what they are doing and discern what need they are trying to fill. Ask them why they like those things. It won't be rational, but it will be telling.

Watch for unhealthy behaviors. So many times the most annoying and unhealthy parts of a person are the very things that point to something really amazing about them. Watch for unhealthy behaviors and imagine what it would look like as redemption for them.

Look for something deeper. When you see excitement or unhealthy behavior, start to think of ways to talk about this area to the young person in a way that gives her autonomy and wide-open, safe spaces to try them. Questions are a great source of challenge within autonomy.

Case Study

In my group, I had a guy who was a self-acknowledged bully. He had a unique ability to know what would really hurt someone the most, and he was heartless in exploiting it. Some of his victims should ask him later in life for compensation for the therapy they will need.

I watched this behavior for months as he bragged about locking kids in dog crates and how he could get online gamers to cry when he played against them. One day, in a moment of safety within our group, he confessed. He acknowledged his behavior and the heart behind it. The weak were his prey. And it wasn't enough to beat them; he had to destroy them so they would never consider retaliation.

My heart was broken for him. This behavior pointed to

some serious wounding that had come from his parents' divorce, the shame of an addicted father and a clueless, enmeshed mother. In that moment, I was able to catch a glimpse of what God had created in him. I wasn't alone, either. One of my youth workers picked up on it immediately.

God used this youth worker to change this young man's life. She asked him what he thought it would be like if, in a year, he had a completely different set of friends because he was their defender instead of their source of pain. We pointed out how God had given him a unique sensitivity to what people felt and how they could be hurt. We challenged him to live as that person we saw and described to him as God's creation. A year later, to everyone's surprise, that is exactly what happened. God changed this guy's heart and even started using him to heal other people's wounds. It began a chain reaction in our group, and it all started with one person's honesty and motivation to change, when he was given the freedom to choose it for himself.

Chapter 5
Specific over Vague

"Good design is making something intelligible and memorable. Great design is making something memorable and meaningful."
—Industrial designer Dieter Rams[16]

"Art distills sensation and embodies it with enhanced meaning in a memorable form —or else it is not art."
—Historian Jacques Barzun[17]

First-year music majors are a sorry group. They throw themselves into a program that instantly reveals everything they are lacking. I remember entering my first year as a jazz major in Auburn University's music department. Instantly, I felt like I was hopeless. Looking around the rest of my fellow music majors, I only saw the things I couldn't do. Finally, I diagnosed myself as having a tin ear. I just couldn't hear the things other students and teachers heard.

My one consolation was music theory class. It was divided into sight singing, theory, and analysis. While I couldn't sight-sing the save my life, theory and analysis saved my stuttering start in studying music. It wasn't until my second year that I realized it, but I have a knack for analysis. As I learned the language of organized sound, I naturally saw my own identity come to life.

Analysis of music is like reading the mind of the dead. In it you study a series of phrases and try to figure out what the composer meant in choosing them. I was hooked from the start. One note could make the difference between a resolving phrase and a deceptive cadence. Heaven appeared before me much like Paul the Apostle's vision. I realized that this was what I was made for.

It wasn't until much later that I saw the benefit of this one character trait. At the time I was serving in a Presbyterian church and was studying the Westminster Catechism. This historic document of the church is a synopsis of the reformed faith. I was trying my best to synthesize it into a meaningful lesson for adolescents. The first question left me stumped. "What is the chief end of man?" it asks. In Presbyterian flare, it answers its own question, "To glorify God and enjoy him forever."

It seems the first lesson from Westminster is, never ask a question that you don't already know the answer to. As I pondered this question, I wondered what it meant to glorify God and enjoy him forever. It seems like a completely true statement, but at the same time seems completely incomplete. How do people glorify God? And how does that lead to enjoying him? My gift for analysis was challenged.

While this question-and-answer from Westminster seems relevant, it has proven to be completely unhelpful to teenagers. It's too vague. How do we glorify God? In asking this of many youth and leaders, I found that we all work towards this goal of "glorifying God," but it hinges on specifics.

Live by the Spirit

When I was thirteen, the Bible confounded me. My faith blossomed as I entered the youth ministry in my church. I had so many questions and a passion to find the answers. I was stymied by the vague teachings I heard though.

In one talk, my youth pastor urged the group to follow Paul's advice in the book of Galatians. The apostle wrote, "live by the Spirit, and you will not gratify the desires of the sinful nature." This, I later realized, was a talk about sex, spawned by a couple caught making out in a car after youth group. The pair raged with hormones and could barely keep their hands off each other. I'm sure the leader giving the lesson thought he'd been clever using the chance to teach and send a message about any wayward displays of affection.

But my sense of curiosity reared its head. It wasn't because of the couple, though. I left wondering what it meant to "live by the Spirit." Was God's Spirit something physical like a house? Maybe I could move next door, and I'd be set. If it was a path, I guess I could walk beside it. That'd work, right?

I was willing to do almost anything to avoid living out the "desires of the sinful nature" that the church had warned me of. I thought of Yoda, "Once you start down the path of the dark side, forever will it dominate your destiny." I definitely didn't want to end up a mouth-breather like Darth Vader.

All night and into the next week I rolled this thought around in my head. There was plenty of room since I wasn't thinking about much of anything else. It must still be echoing inside my skull, because I still wonder about life in the Spirit. What I do know is that very vague phrase did little to describe to me how to accomplish it.

Directions

I have realized that my first attempts at following Paul's advice weren't too far off. Living by the Spirit is very similar to following a path. Only by watching closely as I moved forward would I be able to see God's direction. That's what the Spirit does in this passage.

Can you imagine giving someone directions in the same vague way?

I had that experience while touring around Alabama in an old beat-up Dodge Caravan. Me and four other eager college students volunteered to spend our summer traveling the state ministering to youth in their home churches. We called it Youth Caravan. (I still don't know if it was named after the van or not.)

Somewhere in the great metropolis of Wedowee (population 818), we lost our way. I don't remember where we were coming from or where we were going. What I do remember is the guide whom we asked for directions. He called himself Bert. Bert had a knack for country wisdom and would pepper his directions with phrases that I needed an interpreter for in order to have any hope of understanding.

"What you need to do is go directly down this road and make a turn after a bit. You'll head down a dirt road next to where that great big old oak used to be. No, stick to the side of that road like white on rice 'cause the ditch is slicker than snot on a door knob and Brother Wilson will bless you out if you tear up his new patch of weeds," Bert said, while leaning against a stool in front of the gas station we stopped at.

I tried really hard not to sound sarcastic. Bert really was trying to help. I asked, "How far is "a bit"? And how am I supposed to know where the old oak used to be?

And should I turn right or left?" I'm sure Bert thought I was some kind of alien life form, judging from the way he looked at me. We eventually made it out of Wedowee, despite Bert's help.

I still think of Bert often, though. In the church, you can see a similar problem with direction. Church jargon and simple-answers-to-tough-questions don't leave much room for plotting a course in life. Phrases like "in the world but not of it" and "This world is not my home" summarize different thoughts in living a life of faith, but they fall short of specific help.

I'm going to go out on a limb here, but I bet the young adults you see regularly rarely ask themselves if they are "washed in the blood." They want practical help with the feeling of being lost in their lives. In discipling these young teens, you can't rely on canned answers to their questions. You need to give them specific, turn-by-turn directions.

How It Works

Specifics make the difference between discipleship and education. Where teaching broadcasts knowledge for many people to learn, discipling focuses on the individual. You can teach until you're blue in the face, but until a concept has taken root internally and grows through practice, it has no hope of changing a life.

"Getting to Know You"

This famous line of the Rodgers and Hammerstein song from The King and I sounds a bit like a stalker's lullaby. It's also where the heart of discipleship lives. Without getting to know a teen, you will be unable to give him specific help in her life. With the monosyllabic trends of adolescent dialogue, this is a challenge for youth workers. You can easily run the risk of playing Twenty Questions with a teen you are getting to know.

In this process, you will need some creativity and patience. You have to keep in mind that teens can be very noncommittal when meeting someone new, especially when that person has any authority. Earlier I made a case for da Vinci as a wonderful youth pastor. When it comes to discipleship, the philosopher Socrates would also qualify. His method of questioning grounds my way of knowing teenagers.

Rules for Inquiring Minds

1. *I know that I know nothing.* Socrates used to say this, and it's a good start for those who want to know young adults. Too often, you will look at a teen and start to form opinions before he even starts to talk. Leave those assumptions out of this process. Although you will often see recurring themes in the lives of different young people, each person is unique.

2. *Ask from the open end.* You need to hone your questions into sharpness. Asking a question that can be answered with a "yes" or "no" or just a grunt shuts down this process. Open-ended questions help you get to know a young person. So instead of asking a teen if they like Katy Perry, ask them who their favorite singer is.

3. *You are finite, so let your questions reflect that.* Hidden underneath the skin of the adolescent forehead is a meter that reflects their willingness to answer questions. Early in a relationship, you will only have a couple

of opportunities to ask invasive questions. Keep them limited, or that needle will get into the red zone.

4. *The most important question.* It will always amaze you if you will just ask "Why?" It's the easiest one to remember and the most direct. Though it may feel awkward in the beginning, this one challenging question nets more results than most others.

Seeing a Picture

As you get to know a teenager, you can start seeing what makes them unique. Each answer to your questions is like a brush stroke. Putting those answers together will help you see the big picture of who they are, what motivates them, and what they love. The details fill in the blanks in giving them direction.

Remember that your task here isn't to make new swirls with a brush. God has already created his masterpiece. All you have to do is help a teen see it for herself. Remove the clutter, clean the painting, and display what's left.

You will start to recognize a person's character as you do this. They may be driven by a need for approval or pushed away from friends by a deep shame. These particulars are important. Even the darkest parts of a person show something about how God himself has made that person.

It will be hard, but you must resist the urge to place value on what you learn. Don't judge a teen by his personality. See with God's eyes. The most important part of knowing the details of a young adult's life is creating a place of safety and trust.

Forward Motion

As the picture comes into focus, look for one thing. Early in a relationship, try to pick a unique and admirable trait you have seen and relate it to one of their passions. For example, you might say, "Man, you really rock at playing guitar." These kinds of statements build a foundation for what comes next.

Spend some time letting your disciple hear that you recognize them for something they excel in. Let them absorb that message. Be genuine. Each teen will have her own way of accepting this kind of acknowledgment. Your objective is to see this person as an amazing piece of art.

At some point, you will need to give them an idea of what their gifting could look like. This is the message of God's Kingdom. They belong to something bigger than themselves. God's design for them flows out of understanding who they are in Christ, *specifically*. This may be challenging, but without it, you are not discipling.

As an example, here is the condensed version of an actual conversation that took about 30 minutes: "You have a knack for learning new songs. That requires a lot of self-discipline and determination. I wonder what God would want you to do with that?"

After this kind of a conversation, the young adult may at this point be able to find a path. If so, let him. Likely, he will need specific help. It is critical that he can see at least a next step. You might suggest prayer or a conversation between himself and a friend. Whatever you do, be specific. Give him hope for using his abilities for others.

Case Study

One of the younger teens in a church I served struggled with behavior. He was told all of his life that he had a personality disorder and that controlling his behavior was impossible. I wasn't buying it. Everything I saw in this teen pointed to a lack of discipline.

One theme I see often in youth ministry is the behavioral shift of teens in unstable homes. It doesn't have to be a divorce or severe emotional abuse. Often, it's just a case of neglect. That's what I saw with Terry.

Terry was adopted by an older couple. They wanted to provide a better life for him that would improve his current situation in the state's care. After he was adopted, it became clear that Terry required a lot of attention. The parents struggled to keep up. The father had a thriving business that required a lot of work and the mother had health problems. They loved Terry, but they didn't know how to help him through his frequent outbursts of anger and belligerence.

When Terry acquired junior high status, he started coming to youth group. He was like most typical boys of that age, breaking wind in the middle of discussions and caring little to nothing about personal hygiene. What set him apart was his claim of control. He didn't think he had any. It was commonplace for Terry to be asked to leave the room early in his time with us. I hated doing that, but it became necessary.

After one of his dismissals, Terry and I talked for about ten minutes. He was frustrated with missing the end of the lesson and knew that I wouldn't let him blame anyone but himself. In that conversation, Terry wept. He hated that feeling of anxiousness brought on by being in our room. I realized that he had never been given any help in working with his feelings. Although he saw a psychiatrist regularly, he had never acquired the tools to help him with his feelings.

Together we came up with some very practical responses for Terry. I added a clock to the room so that he could see how much time we had left. We even came up with a secret code for letting him know he was close to being asked to leave the room.

The most amazing part of that conversation came in one acknowledgment. After Terry's confession of anxiety, I saw something special. Terry had an amazing gift for compassion. In fact, that gift often caused a lot of his behavior. He would walk in the room super attuned to how everyone was being treated. Because he was focused on that one trait, he would be hurt when he or one of his friends felt mistreated. It dominated his awareness from that moment on.

After that conversation, I began watching Terry and crediting him with his special gift. I would ask him how people felt after our meetings. Terry now volunteers to pray for everyone after our meetings. It's his special way of caring for our group. This one unique gift helps him to feel like he belongs. It's not just a feeling. He does belong.

When Terry's uniqueness was revealed, he felt significant. He still struggles with behavior, and we have to remind him often that he wants to be present at the end of the meeting to pray. One sentence told me the value of Terry's specific recognition. He said, "I feel like you know me, and that's good."

Discipleship lives in that place of knowing. Only in a deep knowing of a teenager's identity in Christ can those kinds of transformation happen. The specific knowledge informs their sense of worth.

Chapter 6
Personal over Impersonal

"We continue to shape our personality all our life. If we knew ourselves perfectly, we should die."

—Novelist Albert Camus[18]

When I was 19, I had very concrete, passionate dreams of being a rock star. The eighties set the stage for my pilgrimage to personal glory, and I chose guitar as my ride into the spotlight. There's a particular algorithm for achieving success in the late turn of that decade, but it all really boiled down to heavy metal, big hair, and tight pants (preferably with zebra stripes the color of the Aurora Borealis).

Starting at age 15, I practiced my instrument with enthusiasm and gusto. By age 16, I was playing eight hours a day. Somehow, I convinced my parents that I could take the community co-op class at my local high school and give guitar lessons as my job. That meant I got out of school around 10:00 A.M. Industrious, right?

After graduating high school, one of my big breaks included an audition for a band in Nashville. I packed my spandex and hair gel and drove the four-hour trip in what seemed like seconds. Through the years I had made some friends who lived in a house in a suburb of Nashville. It was home to anywhere from 12-19 musicians who were always on the road. We called it the Janice house because of the street it was located on. Sometimes musicians who tour forget details like street names while living the life on the road.

At the time of my visit, there were only three people in residence. Two were good friends who I had worked with before in bands I had played in. Paul was new to me. We shared the same name and both played guitar, a strike against both of us apparently. It wasn't that we didn't get along. In fact, we were very polite to each other. So it wasn't a surprise when Paul burst my bubble.

The third night of my stay in the Janice house, we were all gathered around in a post-meal conversation. Paul, as sincerely as he could be, turned and said to me, "Paul, I just don't like you." All conversation stopped immediately. Suddenly crickets seemed to drown out all other sounds. I was squirming. Trying to force my way out of a really awkward situation, I pretended Paul was making a joke. After all, he did have a dry sense of humor.

So I laughed and said, "Yeah, I thought so."

He continued, "No, seriously. I don't like you. Don't take it personal. No one likes everyone. For me, you're just one of those people I don't like."

It was personal. How could I take it any other way? He didn't say he didn't like my clothes or my guitar. I was the subject of his dislike, and it was definitely personal. The tension of that moment filled the rest of the night. I couldn't just retreat into my room, but there was no escaping the elephant in the room, either.

That exchange taught me a lot about myself. Until then, I thought of myself as a fortress of solitude, not needing any outside encouragement, impervious to criticism. Apparently, I fooled myself. After the dust had settled, I knew something about myself: I needed to be known personally and intimately. My life without someone's specific understanding of who I am feels empty.

Personal

God has always been a personal deity. Before he created anything, he existed in three separate persons. It's an essential element of the Christian faith represented in the creeds and heritage of the church. From the beginning of our relationship to him, he remains close to us, creating us in his image. Personality is an inseparable part of us. We relate to each other and build friendship out of our unique identity. One of my favorite thinkers, Francis Schaeffer, explains it this way:

> *Within the Trinity, before creation of anything, there was real love and real communication. Following on from this statement, the Bible states that God who is personal created man in His own image. A personal God created all things freely in a nondeterminate fashion, and man is created in a special situation—what I would call a special circle of creation. He is the image of this kind of God, and so personality is intrinsic to his makeup. God is personal, and man is also personal.*
> —Francis Schaeffer[19]

It might be impossible for the human mind to hold the tension of a God who created everything and yet wants a relationship with us, personally. The Bible makes it clear this is the case. D. A. Carson makes it plain: "Yet he is personal: he presents himself to us not as raw power or irresistible force, but as Father, as Lord."[20]

You could scour the commentaries of many great thinkers and be fully convinced of this one basic truth about our Lord. He is Father, Son, and Holy Spirit and through these three persons, he approaches us.

Fully assured of this simple truth, you would think that most biblical approaches to discipleship would follow the same model, but you would be wrong. If you've been in youth ministry long, then you have sat through (and maybe been the source of) countless sermons, Bible studies, and small groups that avoid getting personal.

There are reasonable grounds for this. We wouldn't want to offend anybody. We, the leaders, wouldn't want to be too transparent and scare people. Getting into a person's struggles might send them running. All of these safe reasons point to a logical way of leadership, but this wasn't Jesus' way.

Reading the Gospels, you will hear story after story of Jesus getting personal. He puts people on the spot. Often he would confront people about their deepest shame after just meeting them. The Son of God had no shame in getting real with people, and he didn't wait until they were comfortable enough for him to jump into their emotional junk.

Jesus' way of discipleship is personal. Generic challenges to a moral code, while true, are useless in helping teens live their faith. Telling them not to go out and party this weekend has no impact without knowing their individual struggles and giving them help tailored just for them.

Fixing Problems

Early in my marriage, I realized something about my nature. I'm arrogant. Really arrogant. This became obvious one night as my wife and I talked about our day. It was a common ritual for us to unpack our time apart. At the time, my wife had some challenges at work. In sharing these, I would interrupt her with occasional comments like, "You should have..." or "They need to..." After a while, my wife (very patiently) explained to me that what worked for me wouldn't always work for her.

It was a revelation. My solutions, though well meant and thought out, didn't account for her individual nature. In fact, my desire to solve her problems only conveyed the idea that she couldn't solve them herself.

This idea of personal ministry doesn't look like problem-solving each teenager's problems. Instead, it enters into their specific situation and asks them what they would do about it. It might include instruction or suggested tools for working through issues, but it leaves room for them to choose a path. The danger in personal ministry to young adults lies in a domineering leader. The goal isn't to solve their problems but to help them find better solutions.

How It Works

I often wish I had Jesus' power of discernment. That way I could get to the point after knowing someone for exactly .2 seconds. Unfortunately, I am a finite guy with all of my own challenges and problems. Ministering personally is a constant study of objective listening.

Listening

You have probably heard a little about listening. Your parents probably lectured you about the difference between listening and hearing, as an exercise in understanding what enters your ears. They were right, of course. There is a difference between audible sounds and understanding.

In discipleship, listening involves understanding that comes from an interaction between a person and the Holy Spirit. A simple dialogue between two people can be taken at face value. Maybe it's about the weather or a seemingly innocent subject, but underneath the words are a deeper meaning.

Heeding a call from a young adult takes practice, but it can be easily developed. You can hear the deeper message underneath their words. When I was younger, I remember hearing that deeper message in the words of a potential love interest. We met through a mutual friend at a transitional moment between other courtships. She had just cut her hair in a very short style that I would later learn was a rebellion against her former boyfriend. She told me, "I've just cut my hair off, and I'm not sure I like it."

It was just a compound sentence. Underneath the words, though, she was asking a question. What she wanted to know was, did I like her despite her new hairstyle? It was one of the first times I was aware of a deeper meaning under the surface of a conversation. Looking back, I was aware of so many other times I had missed the true meaning of a heart-to-heart message.

Later in youth ministry I would hear so much more in these exchanges. "I'm a little weird" equals "Do you accept me?"

Listening requires us to understand, if only partially, a person's feelings, thoughts, and beliefs. It responds to those feelings with assurance, provides understanding to their thoughts, and confirms beliefs.

Detachment

This part can be really short and sweet. You have to be able to detach yourself from the teens you listen to. Not being able to do this, in the counseling world, is called transference. It happens when a counselor hears a client and transfers his own feelings into the conversation. This is the opposite of listening since it taints the message with the perspective of the hearer. Mental detachment allows you to listen without imparting your own ideas on the speaker's revelation.

What this looks like in real life resembles a pane of glass. I'm picturing visitation in a jail where two people try to talk to each other through a transparent barrier. You have probably seen this in a movie or on TV. The glass protects each person from harm and prevents anything dangerous from being passed from one person to another.

You can see its usefulness in a penal situation, but listening with a similar virtual barrier has many of the same benefits.

Being emotionally detached protects both the teller and the listener. It makes safe anything the person sharing says, since the reaction of the listener is limited. Too much of an emotional response from someone receiving can limit the freedom in talking. Likewise, the person listening is protected from overly empathizing with the message of the other person. They can be more objective and hear more clearly.

Listening with detachment might invoke an idea of harshness or callousness. In fact, it works in the opposite way. When each person feels free from emotional fallout in a conversation, each person is more able to say what might otherwise be harmful. The gist is that detachment opens a space for freedom that builds protection in a relationship.

Flow

When you can listen objectively and detach yourself from a young adult's emotional backdrop, you're ready for a big adventure. Much of what I do in the way of discipleship I learned from a Hungarian psychology professor named Mihaly Csikszentmihalyi. His name looks like a mouthful, but really isn't. As fast as you can, say, "Me hay, chick sent me hay." After practice, this will either start to sound natural or like raising phlegm from your throat.

Csikszentmihalyi is known for his work as a psychologist specifically working on the human perspective of creativity and happiness. I was introduced to him through his book *Flow: The Psychology of Optimal Experience.*

> *The optimal state of inner experience is one in which there is order in consciousness. This happens when psychic energy—or attention—is invested in realistic goals, and when skills match the opportunities for action. The pursuit of a goal brings order in awareness because a person must concentrate attention on the task at hand and momentarily forget everything else.*
> —Mihaly Csikszentmihalyi[21]

You might be wondering what this person with an unthinkable name has to do with discipleship, but stick with me. Teenagers live in a world of trying to achieve goals. Unfortunately, they go about achieving those goals in a self-defeating way. I call it the Tiger Woods syndrome. Many people are inspired after watching the golfer, Tiger Woods, win a game of golf. He's an artist, pitching from the rough with a 3-wood, hitting with only the blade of a wedge to give a low-flying ball and generally using his creativity to give himself an edge.

After seeing these amazing feats of golf mastery, you get the itch to enrich our life with a round of golf. It really is a good walk spoiled. After seeing Tiger, you want to re-enact his brilliance. So you try to perform the amazing shots you saw him make. It never works. After eight holes, you're ready to tuck your tail and quit. Obviously you don't have whatever Tiger has. Giving up seems the only reasonable option.

What you missed was the countless hours of practice everyday. You want to jump to the end result instead of taking the time to learn the techniques. Csikszentmihalyi uses a process to take us from a limited skill set to mastery. He suggests setting an ultimate goal and then building the daily practices that will eventually lead to that ultimate prize (See flow diagram at http://beingministry. com/wp-content/uploads/2012/09/Flow.gif).

Each small step up the channel is called Flow. It's the small steps that build something great. Those steps have to be challenging enough to maintain interest without creating too much anxiety. If a task is too easy, you get bored; and if it's too hard, you get frustrated. A tailored plan meets you where you are and moves you forward towards competence. Through the use of Flow, you gain a sense of accomplishment.

Synergy

Using Flow, you combine listening and detachment to work with a young adult to help her progress in maturity. These form the tripod of personal direction. Listening without detachment creates a superimposed expectation on a disciple. Getting personal without giving direction ends without change. Finally, direction with some form of personal, self-direction is just veiled control. All three of these techniques bind together the value of getting personal in discipling young people.

Case Study

Sometimes I have to scratch my head and wonder at the teenagers God brings into my life. Vicky was one of those. The very first meeting she attended, I couldn't believe how backward her beliefs were. Honestly, I didn't think she would come back night after night, but she did. She always told me something that was going on in her life that was causing her grief or joy. Either seemed fine most of the time.

About six months into Vicky's time with the youth ministry, she had a dilemma. While sleeping at a friend's house, she got caught sneaking back in through the doggie door of the house at around 5 A.M. Her friend's mother was not impressed with her. Neither were her friends, who had snuck out earlier and come home around 3. Vicky was in a world of trauma.

I received lots of calls the next morning, and most were from the host mother. When Vicky called, she wanted advice on what to tell her parents. I suggested that she tell them everything. As scared as she was, she did it. It was an amazing time for her. Her parents grounded her for maybe the first time, but she felt cleansed.

From then on, Vicky's life reports were regular and mostly inspiring. As she came to the end of her high school career, someone asked me what her secret was. I thought about that for a long time. What was her secret? Looking back, I think she wasn't afraid, after that confession with her parents, to get personal.

From the time she confronted her past, she was free to give the deepest, darkest details of her life. She reminds me of Ian Malcolm from *Jurassic Park* who was described as having an excessive personality. What happened with Vicky came through her realizing who she was and being willing to talk openly about it. She probably grew more spiritually and emotionally than any other student I have worked with.

That's the power of personal. It risks more and reaps more benefits. Transparency shows through to the core of a person willing to be personal. Young adults like Vicky live on a different level than others who hide their personalities. Because she was willing to show her truest self, Vicky will always be one of those cherished people in my ministry experience.

Chapter 7
Internal Value over External Value

"It's not what goes into your mouth that defiles you; you are defiled by the words that come out of your mouth."

—Jesus (Matthew 15:11, NLT)

"You're on a path to become just like your father."

Knowing the context of that statement probably changes its meaning. The father was a known drunk who had recently lost the family's substantial livelihood. There had been no intimacy with his wife and family for years. Only a need to exist near him had kept the family together. Now, all of that crumbled around them.

The son who heard that sentence was sitting next to me on a couch. His eyes glazed with fury as he acknowledged its truth. At only 17, he had become an addict burying his pain in alcohol and drugs. Outwardly, he was a prince, but inside he felt like a beggar. No matter how much he succeeded in everyone's eyes, he still felt like a failure. His life felt meaningless.

Only one thing remained for this lost son: the desire to distinguish himself. Until that conversation, it hadn't mattered what endeavor he tried, he just had to succeed.

The fruit of that time together still grows in his life. A seed was planted that, when nourished, still brings forth shoots of leaves and branches to hold new life. The seed is value. Never before had the lost son been able to see himself as anything worthy. He lived with the constant need to excel in life and prove his worth. Success after success never filled the need he felt. It was a bottomless pit.

The only peace he found was in playing guitar. When he played, all he thought about was the next note and the feeling of playing a song to perfection. Something inside him knew a great joy in his playing. The only measure he accepted was his own idea of the song. This was the freedom he felt and needed to survive. It was also where he found God.

Value

This story sounds like many you have probably heard in youth ministry. It certainly could be a subtext for the story of the prodigal son. When I read this story, I wonder what could have driven the wayward son to ask for his inheritance. He essentially is telling his father that he wished his father were dead. Did he hate his father so much or was it just greed?

The prodigal son sets out to live a different life. Jesus tells us that he squandered his wealth. Likely he spent most of it to impress others. Whether he did or not, this present-day son I was working with would have made the same choice. They both wanted something they felt like their fathers couldn't give them. They both had something to prove to themselves and everyone around them.

How often do you see this in youth ministry? Teenagers long to impress their parents, their friends, and anyone in their general vicinity, all while pretending they don't care. In our culture, this trait is nurtured to instill the drive to succeed. You can see it in the race for academic perfection or organized sports and even within families. My own daughters, with no prompting from parents, race for the stairs to our house so that they can be first to get into the car. They still do this at age seven and eight. Something in us strives to be first.

The fruits of this race are fickle though. To feel good about yourself, you always have to win. When you don't win, you're lumped in with the losers— a lesser class of people who just didn't work hard enough. What a trap. What a lie.

The Apostle Paul uses this imagery as well, and from our perspective, it seems to fit. "Run to win" (1 Corinthians 9:14) he tells us. "I will be proud that I did not run the race in vain and that my work was not useless" (Philippians 2:16), Paul also writes. And finally, "let us run with endurance the race God has set before us" (Hebrews 12:1).

It seems that God put us here to compete, but I don't think he meant us to compete against each other. The race we run is within us. It's the path we take to define ourselves through either the world's idea of success or God's. Chasing the world's approval is much more like chasing the wind. It's a never-ending pursuit of a false perfection depending on a fickle group of people. God's idea of success runs in the opposite direction.

How It Works

Discipling a teenager is like trying to do brain surgery. My father always thought doctors had an easy job compared to fixing cars. His perspective was that the human body is pretty self-repairing. With most illness, it will probably just get better on its own. Cars don't do that. They cave in to entropy sooner or later. I once related my father's opinion to an open-heart surgeon who smiled and said, "Tell him to try to fix a car while it is being driven down the road!"

Most young adults will struggle with the source of their value all of their lives. When they realize they are getting it from one place that is not sustaining, they will move to another equally detrimental, or at least unhelpful, self-value. Like cars, they won't get better without serious work and constant maintenance.

It's easy for adolescents to become trapped by their values. They have the dual nature of wanting to be an individual while also needing to fit in. You can see them skate along the edge of both needs. They gather in groups sharing the same taste in music, clothes, and hairstyles. When you look closely though, there are slight variations.

The trap comes from those who try too hard to gain acceptance. They change their look or preferences so that others will like them. When they are accepted, it is only for what they changed. Their true selves aren't the reason for belonging. Instead, they feel like a part of the group because of what they put on over their identity. The worst part of this scenario is that they know it.

Value has to come from within. When it is based on externals, it becomes subjective to the many opinions of other people.

Recognition

You will have to find what a young disciple values most in life to start. For some it's relationships, for others it's clothes. It doesn't matter what they use to make themselves feel good, you just need to be able to see it.

Linus has his blanket. The Lone Ranger had his horse. Katy Perry has her past. Where would they be without them? As you get to know a student, watch for those things that they always focus on. They probably couldn't tell you themselves what they carry around with them that gives them worth, but you will see it by its consistent presence.

When I worked at a church in Orlando, I met a student who always had a set of headphones on. These weren't the meager ear buds that other teens would wear, either. These cans always rested on his collarbones with the wire hanging down somewhere into another dimension. I never saw where the wire came from. Two things struck me after knowing him for a while. He was never without those headphones, and they were never on his ears.

One day I asked him what kind of music he liked. Shrugging, he looked at me through a squint and a grin. So I pressed further, "What's the last thing you listened to on your headphones?" Nothing. No response. Blank.

Only after this conversation did I realize the truth. He didn't listen to music. The headphones were silent. They were an accessory of his persona. His value came from being known for loving music.

What he really loved was concerts. It didn't matter what style of music from string quartets to screamo, he loved the play of instruments from an artist's hands. After prying for an eternity, he produced an iPod from his too tight, skinny jeans. It was full of live performances that he never listened to because they weren't magical anymore.

The real work began after that recognition. My mission: find out what made live music amazing to this guy.

That's the work of recognizing value. It looks at the surface and finds what's underneath.

Worth

Worth is a funny thing. The dictionary tells you its "equivalent in value to the sum or item specified." You know from experience what these words don't say. Worth never rests. It's a fluid thing that slips through fingers like sand. Most teenagers live in a world of the shifting sands of worth.

Fashions come and go leaving piles of clothes in their wake. Legwarmers were once the height of fashion. The one-time uniform of professional dancers, who cut off socks to keep their legs warm while freeing their feet for dance, became the to-die-for attire for aerobics in the eighties. Now, you can't give them away. Most eighties' throwbacks will get you beat up in gym class, or at least cause societal banishment.

Underneath fashion trends, though, is the desire to express yourself and be accepted. The student with the headphones knew this. He was known throughout his school for loving music. It defined his worth to his peers. Unfortunately, most worth comes from an outside source. Value doesn't work that way. It comes from a place hidden within you.

Values

Some philosophers would say values come from the heart. Maybe that's true. They have to come from somewhere. In our society though, it's easy to confuse values with outcomes. Most people live their lives trying to get the desired outcome, whatever that is. Maybe it's a better house or shinier car. Those are outcomes. Values direct people to life on their terms.

Climber Ivon Chouinard, founder of the clothing company Patagonia, lives by values, not goals. Instead of trying to become a business mogul, he just wants to make gear that he can use to do the things he loves. What he loves just happens to be climbing and surfing and being outdoors.

> *I've been a student of Zen philosophy for many years. In Zen archery, for example, you forget about the goal—hitting the bull's eye—and instead focus on all the individual movements involved in shooting an arrow. You practice your stance, reaching back and smoothly pulling an arrow out of the quiver, notching it on a string, controlling your breathing, and letting the arrow release itself. If you've perfected all the elements, you can't help but hit the center of the target. The same philosophy holds true for climbing mountains. If you focus on the process of climbing, you'll end up on the summit.*
>
> —Ivon Chouinard[22]

I love Chouinard's practice. He doesn't consider the goal. Instead he focuses himself on the joy of the process. It's an internal sense of accomplishment of doing what you love. I would be willing to bet that he would continue to fire arrow after arrow even if he hit nothing, just for the feeling of letting the arrow release itself.

Teens in American society have been taught to reach for the goal. It's so inherent that you probably don't even think about it. From grades to sports to line leaders, children are taught that the best thing is a win.

Winning is great, don't get me wrong. But the win isn't the best thing in life. Better than a win is the satisfaction of knowing what you love and doing it. That only comes from internal awareness. Values describe that inner voice that only you can hear.

Case Study

Wren was the most driven teen I knew. He was in the top of his class, an athlete, and musician. Everything he did seemed to be a success. When he made a CD with a friend and sold it at a local fast-food restaurant and made more than $500, I wasn't surprised. Or when he used his father's credit card to buy concert tickets to sell to friends, it didn't seem odd. He had a plan and could make it happen.

For some reason though, he never seemed to think that anything was good enough. Outwardly, he looked like any happy young person, but inwardly, he struggled with himself. He just didn't think he was that big of a deal.

One day, Wren and I picked up a Milo's hamburger. As we ate I started asking him about his future. What did he want to do after college? What were his plans? He couldn't answer any of my questions. I finally gave up, much to his relief. That lasted about ten seconds. Wren had no idea what he wanted to do. All of the activities he involved himself in were to impress other people in his life.

Realizing this, I asked him what he loved to do. Again, I got nowhere. So I took a risk. After leaving the restaurant, I asked, "Wren, tell me five things about yourself that you love." Silence choked the conversation to death. There was nothing Wren could come up with.
Sadly, Wren resembles a lot of teens you work with. He

has no idea of what he loves to do. Instead, he settles for impressing his peers by outperforming them. Performance is an empty goal. Someone else will always outperform you. There's no joy in it.

Watching someone do what he loves is different, though. A craftsman using a plane to slowly shave off the side of a door. A musician who loses herself in hours of practice simply because she loves to play. These people enjoy life because the source of their values is clear.

Paul the Apostle tells us that we are masterpieces created to do amazing things. You won't find out what those things are without taking the inner path. Everything else pales in comparison to knowing what you are created to do and doing it.

Chapter 8
Implicit over Explicit

"The majority of important things cannot be said outright," Elodin said. "They cannot be made explicit. They can only be implied."

—Patrick Rothfuss[23]

"In fact, in his public ministry he never taught without using parables; but afterward, when he was alone with his disciples, he explained everything to them."

—Jesus (Mark 4:34, NLT)

"The true color of life is the color of the body, the color of the covered red, the implicit and not explicit red of the living heart and the pulses. It is the modest color of the unpublished blood."

—Poet Alice Meynell[24]

Sometimes you hear stories in youth ministry that make you want to cry. Ben had one of those. As I sat in our regular youth meeting, I saw a young man sitting upright, making eye contact, leaning into the discussion, on the edge of his seat—dissolve into a little boy lying in a fetal position, staring into oblivion. If his body language were a mood ring, it would be solid black.

The rest of the teenagers in the room either didn't notice the change in Ben's posture, or maybe they felt too uncomfortable to comment. Small blessings. What just happened? I remember we were talking about family and the role of parents. The connection was made to the epic life God created us to live, and what that looked like for each person. Going around the room, I made deliberate eye contact with each person in the room. Suddenly Ben was facing away and practically in a puddle on the floor.

In my head, I started running through the conversations I had with Ben while playing video games. He was a nervous guy with a jittery composure and frequent eye twitches. I found out when he came on a retreat with us that he was on several medications. He had never spent the night away from home. In fact, if rumors were true, he used to sleep outside his parents door hoping they wouldn't leave while he was asleep.

After our meeting I was tempted to find Ben and have a talk. I wanted to make sure he was all right. I wanted to help him. As much as I tried to build him up though, he would deflate in front on me. He was like a deflated balloon. Any kind of specific encouragement or affirmation seemed to produce only shame. He just couldn't receive direct praise at all.

Stumped, I called a close friend who also was an amazingly gifted counselor. He listened to Ben's story and helped me understand a different way to help Ben. Ben had a lifetime of shame that served as the backdrop of all his interactions with people. No matter what those people said, he would balance the scales in his mind. If they complimented him, he would think he had tricked them. If they cut him down, he would think they misunderstood him completely. His contempt could swing back and forth directed at himself or another to always keep himself away from meaningful relationships. That's when I started using implicit communication.

Before I would be as explicit as I could in trying to build Ben up. If he won a round of Halo, I would say, "Way to go! You beat all of us." Judging by his demeanor, Ben was telling himself he got lucky. Implicit language handles the same scenario in a completely different way.

The first time I tried this new technique was the day after Ben and one of his friends caught a case of the giggles in one of our gatherings. We've all been there. It's the worst time to laugh, and that fact alone makes it impossible to stop. Only, this time, I could see it ending, and then Ben manufacturing an extra five minutes of chuckles. Several others in our group confirmed it.

So the next day Ben apologized for disrupting our time saying he just couldn't control himself. Now I could have just lectured him or forgiven him, but instead I tried something different. I asked, "Well, did you have problems controlling yourself as a little boy?" Ben's smile drifted off his face. Slightly confused, he asked me what I meant. I asked him, implying that only little boys have a problem with self-control, how he was able to finally stop. He wouldn't answer me. I saw the war going on inside him. As the conversation continued, I was able to brag on Ben for being a man. I told him I was impressed that he could find the strength to stop. Men can take themselves in hand, right? All of the language was implicit, and that began my use of indirect communication.

How It Works

Language

"Some things have to be believed to be seen."
—Madeleine L'Engle[25]

If you work with adolescents, you probably spend a fair amount of time watching what you say. There are the subjects we know we shouldn't stray into. Conversations that are adult-themed or too personal have to be watched closely. Some subjects we are certain need to come up. Life and faith and how they work together to help them through their struggles. Maybe you've heard that 83 percent of all communication is nonverbal. Implicit language lives somewhere in that part of conversation where you know that something is certain, but you can't remember how you came by that knowledge. Researcher Paul Watzlawick says, "There exist, then, certain language forms that enable us to say something without quite saying it."[26]

In Watzlawick's research, you find how the brain interprets language to find meaning. As an example he uses the comic strip called *The Born Loser*. One suited man says to another, "So you're quitting to join Sidney Winecoop and Associates?" The second man replies, "Check!" The first man then says, "Well, that should raise the level of intelligence in both companies!" The implicit message is two-fold. First, the second man's absence will make the original company better, therefore he's an idiot. Second, Sidney Winecoop and Associates are even greater idiots than you.

This is a very negative, manipulative way to communicate, but there are just as many positive ways to use implicit language.

"Try to overeat just enough so that you will lose between three and four pounds per week" or "As a result of your self-hypnosis, eating will become for you a pleasure the like of which you have never experienced before. The smallest quantity of food will taste so much better and fulfill (homophony will fill, satiate, but also with "fulfilling your wish to lose weight") you so much more than large meals did ever before....

—Paul Watzlawick[27]

In this example, you see how the implied message of overeating gives the message of power and control of consumption. Explicitly, it acknowledges and gives permission to overeating. The implicit message hints at the ability to eat "just enough" to control weight gain. The second example speaks of being full but hinges on the implied message of taste. Implicit language might seem complicated right now, but listen to yourself for a week. You will almost surely see how you are already using it daily.

Story

Stories are the most obvious use of implicit language. They aren't always clearly rational or succinct, but they tell us things that reason can't. Myths tell about heroic deeds and villainy unlike the shortened versions with just the facts. Movies like *The Matrix*, *Lord of the Rings*, and *Star Wars* point to themes that have always been popular. A common person discovers that they are part of something larger than themselves. They are important and needed.

These themes resonate with our very basic needs. Stories convey that meaning better than a pronouncement of them. Telling someone out right that they are important and needed just doesn't carry the weight that a story does. That's why we love them. Even short stories or phrases have the power to move us.

Proverbs summarize complex ideas and hint at further understanding. I once had a teen say, after reading the Bible extensively for ten minutes, that he now had a favorite verse. He proudly related it to me as if my very existence would be threatened without it. He reported, "Eat honey my son, for it is good." I think he was probably joking, but I couldn't stop thinking about it. The factual content of that proverb gives permission to eat honey, but implied in it is the idea that we should take time to enjoy the good things of this life. I knew something more about life because of that proverb.

Neil Gaiman reminds me often of the power of stories. He writes, "Fairy tales, as G. K. Chesterton once pointed out, are not true. They are more than true. Not because they tell us that dragons exist, but because they tell us they can be defeated."[28]

Language is the vehicle for meaning in your life. Stories stir something deeper within us that we can't often articulate with just the facts. "Stories are equipment for living," writes Barbara Myerhoff in her book with the similar name, and she's right on course. Story is what you tune in to on a Friday night on the TV, what you read until the wee hours of the morning, and what you are asked about when you come home from work.

Precedent

You might be wondering if this is right or ethical to use implicit language in your relationships. Hopefully you can see a bit of it in your life already. It may seem wrong not to come out and say things as directly as possible, but the Bible tells us that Jesus often used implicit language in his ministry.

"Jesus used many similar stories and illustrations to teach the people as much as they could understand. In fact, in his public ministry he never taught without using parables; but afterward, when he was alone with his disciples, he explained everything to them."
—Mark 4:33-34, NLT

Using parables, Jesus was able to talk about the kingdom of God in a way that was confusing for some. Some people missed the meaning. Even his own disciples often had to be clued in later. In the story of the woman caught in adultery, Jesus says yes while meaning no.

As he was speaking, the teachers of religious law and the Pharisees brought a woman who had been caught in the act of adultery. They put her in front of the crowd.

"Teacher," they said to Jesus, "this woman was caught in the act of adultery. The law of Moses says to stone her. What do you say?"

They were trying to trap him into saying something they could use against him, but Jesus stooped down and wrote in the dust with his finger. They kept demanding an answer, so he stood up again and said, "All right, but let the one who has never sinned throw the first stone!" Then he stooped down again and wrote in the dust.

When the accusers heard this, they slipped away one by one, beginning with the oldest, until only Jesus was left in the middle of the crowd with the woman.
—John 8:3-9 NLT

Jesus explicitly gives his conditional consent to stone the woman. The implied message though is they can't do it. Anyone who hasn't sinned can throw a stone. In this interaction, we see Jesus teaching an important truth through indirect language.

What really happened there was a use of two separate pieces of knowledge that are linked. Jesus could have just told the crowd they had no right to judge the woman because of their own sin. That would have likely become a shouting match about the law. In fact, any disagreement with the crowd at all would have probably ended in at least one stoning. So Jesus agrees with them. Yes, the law does give them the justification to stone this woman.

How It Works

Ok, so Jesus used implicit language to guide people into hearing messages they couldn't explicitly accept. How do you do it? There are some really simple ways to start. To understand implicit language, you have to understand the way the mind works. The Heath brothers explain what many people have known for years.

The conventional wisdom in psychology, in fact, is that the brain has two independent systems at work at all times. First, there's what we called the emotional side. It's the part of you that is instinctive, that feels pain and pleasure. Second, there's the rational side, also known as the reflective or conscious system. It's the part of you that deliberates and analyzes and looks into the future.
—Chip Heath and Dan Heath[29]

Our emotions are the place where implied messages live. They speak to us about our worries and fears. We aren't consciously aware of much of what happens there, but it affects our lives just the same.

Thoughts are more in the front of our minds, and they explain all the surface-level happenings of our lives. The Heath brothers liken these two parts of us to an Elephant and Rider. The Rider is our reason that gives direction through life. The Elephant, the bigger, stronger part of us, represents our emotions.

If you want to change things, you've got to appeal to both. The Rider provides the planning and direction, and the Elephant provides the energy. So if you reach the Riders of your team but not the Elephants, team members will have understanding without motivation. If you reach their Elephants but not their Riders, they'll have passion without direction. In both cases, the flaws can be paralyzing.

—Chip Heath and Dan Heath[30]

Implicit language appeals to the Elephant through the awareness of the Rider.

Think about a person with a struggle. What is it they most want to be convinced of? The obvious ones jump out. Girls want to be told they are beautiful, guys that they are handsome, teens that they can have authority, etc. You get the picture. Let's start with women. You can't just tell them they are beautiful. It's too vague and meaningless, and they will deny it nine times out of ten. It would be great if the right words rolled out of a guy's mouth at exactly the right time, but that rarely happens either.

Many women want to be complimented and yet struggle with accepting compliments. You could say, "You're a lot less ugly than the other girls." but that probably wouldn't win over a girl's heart. Instead you might try, "You shouldn't be embarrassed of your beauty." In this message, you still describe her as beautiful, but the implicit message addresses her discomfort or disbelief in her own beauty.

Synthesis

Synthesis combines several items to make something new. The best vehicle for this is figurative language. It takes a picture of a situation and describes it from another, limited perspective. Read the next paragraph aloud.

There, three four houses, a run-down inn, I enter, the
wine is unsurpassed, summer's essence, days of bronze
and of black ornament, salamander gorge, I ask for
some names, laughter,... a dog barks, the sun floats in
the metallic blue of the phosphorus cliffs, the bells toll,
I see the priest, black figure, black figure of ink, black
figure of ink and black laughter, running across the road,
greeting....

—Heinz Weder[31]

This grouping of words breaks so many rules of
grammar it should be arrested by a gaggle of professors
from Stanford University. What it lacks in following the
understood rules of language it makes up for in creating
a mood and feel of what it describes. It pulls you into the
world it portrays. This is classic figurative language used
to evoke an image in the reader. These images created
in figurative language can be infinitely more powerful in
appealing to the heart of a disciple.

Knowing this, it shouldn't surprise us that parables
were a major teaching tool for Jesus. Jesus uses the parable of the leaven and the mustard seed to teach how the
kingdom of heaven starts small then grows to be enor-
mous. The parables of the hidden treasure and the pearl
illustrate the value of God's kingdom. The lost sheep, the
lost coin, and the prodigal son point to loss and redemption.

These teachings were common for Jesus and his disciples. When you look at the audience of each parable,
though, it tells a deeper story. The leaven and mustard
seed parables were told to the multitudes, probably close
to Jesus' home. The audience for the hidden treasure and
the lost sheep are likely similar. Jesus' teaching on the
lost son though had particular listeners in mind.

In the Gospel of Luke, this parable is set on the backdrop of the tax collectors, sinners, and Pharisees. Knowing the hearers, it seems clear that Jesus was using a parable and implicit language to speak to each group. The "sinners" were the prodigal son, exemplifying the heart of the rejected people. The other son is obviously the Pharisees, who feel entitled to something more for their faithfulness.

Drifting

Breathing exchanges gases in the body's life to sustain it. Encouragement works similarly in youth ministry. Encouragement breathes life into student ministry. As it passes from one person to another, it creates trust and safety. Some teenagers aren't able to receive direct encouragement. Something about them disbelieves any affirming word they are given.

> *You meet a girl: shy, unassuming. If you tell her she's beautiful, she'll think you're sweet, but she won't believe you... But there's a better way. You show her she is beautiful. You make mirrors of your eyes, prayers of your hands against her body. It is hard, very hard, but when she truly believes you... Suddenly the story she tells herself in her own head changes. She transforms. She isn't seen as beautiful. She is beautiful, seen.*
> —Patrick Rothfuss[32]

Young adults often disbelieve both criticism and praise. They wonder about the hidden meanings underneath the actual words. They think of implied meanings as self-seeking manipulation. But like most tools of the enemy, this one proves useful in restoring emotional and spiritual health to young people.

Using implicit language reminds me of the Pixar

movie *Cars*. Race car Lightning McQueen is stranded in a remote town along Route 66. The local authority gives him a chance to be free. A race. All he has to do is beat an old, rundown car on a dirt track. He fails miserably. In one turn, he over-steers and crashes into a thorny patch along the side of the track. The old-timer tells him he has to turn right to go left. Later he realizes the physics of drifting. Drifting is when a car's rear wheels lose traction, allowing them to slide sideways while keeping control on the front wheels.

Using implicit language feels a lot like drifting. Often your natural instinct will be to talk to students in a direct way. Many of them are unable to fully receive what you say, both in correction and praise, especially early in a relationship. Later you can get to some direct communication, but it will likely be easier in the beginning to use some backwards driving until then.

Playing Opposites

Part of the beauty in using implicit language is the surprise of hearing what you didn't expect. Jesus did this so often you just wonder if he didn't sit around thinking of comebacks all the time. Remember when the religious leaders asked him about paying taxes? They thought they had him trapped. He turned it into an object lesson using a fish. Jesus seems to never have had that lingering synopsis of a conversation ending with, "I should gave said...." Implicit language works in much the same way. You can often use it best when trying to say the opposite of what people expect.

I don't remember where I heard this story first, but it reminds me of what I can do with expectations. Two men, an American and a Middle Eastern, were traveling together on flight. After the initial discussion wound down, the American asked where the other man was going. He explained that he was going to pick up a bride.

The American thought that was a peculiar thing to do, so he asked for more details. The Middle Eastern gentleman told him that everyone from his part of the world pays a high price for their brides, pointing out that, unlike Americans, they value their wives. Thinking he'd found a place of superiority, he asked the American how much he paid for his wife. The American replied that he couldn't buy a bride for only money. He had to give her money and shelter, emotional support, love, kindness, gentleness, and on and on he went. Basically, he had to share everything with her.

It realigned the conversation. Now when thinking of a bride, the Middle Eastern man would think about how much he would give his bride. Using implicit language realigns expectations, and more importantly, assumptions. It goes into the places where direct language can't, pulling out deeper meanings.

Case Study

On September 25, 2007, I experienced an interruption in my normal time of discipleship. My regular group of guys I met with suddenly disappeared. Later I realized that this interruption coincided with the release of *Halo 3*. They were completely and immediately unavailable for anything else. On a rare occasion, I caught one of them through the now-standard tool in ministry known as texting.

After punishing my thumbs for ten minutes, I got a date set for him and the other guys to come meet and play *Halo 3* at the church. Controversy abounded in the church at the time about playing M-rated games. Our guys were all playing it anyway, so I took a gamble. Three guys showed up the first day. I hooked up a projector and sound system, and after an hour of gameplay, my ears rung until the next morning.

When they left, they asked if they could bring a couple of friends next time. I told them, "Sure!" The next week there were 13, and the weeks following, we had waiters for pickup games of sixteen. That's when I met Eric.

Eric was a quiet guy who dressed nicely and had polite manners. That is, until you put an Xbox 360 controller in his hand. Then he came alive like Frankenstein after a few gigawatts of electricity. It's amazing how effective video games are in discipleship. Maybe it's because the time to talk is brief, or that there isn't the pressure of facing someone while playing. Either way, I got to know Eric against the backdrop of explosions and victory chants. Eric began coming to our youth group after playing gaming with us for a couple of weeks.

Although he was polite, Eric had a sadistic side. His winning celebrations would demean and shame other players. I had to intervene more than once when he went so far I thought someone might cry. As I began to understand him more, I realized that Eric had been severely abused. I couldn't say specifically what kind of abuse it was, but the symptoms all pointed to some trauma that he never healed from. He didn't like anyone to touch him, ever. Though he was quick verbally, he shied away from physical confrontation. All evidence pointed to physical or sexual abuse, or maybe both.

Because of the shame of abuse and Eric's personality, I knew I couldn't ask direct questions about his past. If I were too explicit in getting his history, he would take off, never to be seen at our gatherings again. Fortunately, Eric's mother would pick him up, usually last from our youth group times. I started asking Eric basic questions about his family. I was shut down for months before I even learned his father's profession.

That's when I began using stories. I started out telling stories that related to a topic for Bible study. Shortly after that, I started telling stories about average people overcoming their problems. I could see a little spark in Eric's eyes when I told those. He would suddenly be leaning on the edge of his seat, eyes focused on a stray piece of lint on the floor. He was engaged, but distant at the same time. Looking back, I think it probably felt safe for him.

I wish I could say that I got to the bottom of Eric's abuse, but that never happened. He just kept coming back and became more involved in our little group. Sometimes he was more distant than others. I wondered if he was still trying to resolve his past. What happened through this time was a gradual opening up in Eric. He would share more with our group about the things in his life. I thought this was normal until another guy in our group said Eric never talked about himself. He felt safer with others and more willing to be known.

This might seem anticlimactic to some leaders, but for youth leaders, this is gold. You rarely see the end result of your work with teenagers. Small shifts are about all you can hope for. Eric had one of those shifts. It came through an unconfessed dragon in his past that he had the hope of conquering through stories about others.

Chapter 9
Praxis

"Not all who wander are lost."

—J. R. R. Tolkein[33]

I made a bad habit of taking my two daughters to Target every Tuesday when I picked them up from school. We usually had only a couple of items to buy, apple juice or shampoo or a new movie, but we would always traverse the whole store in a slow window-shopping ramble.

One day, we made it through with only a small bag of Hass avocados. My kryptonite in stores is in picking a line to checkout. No matter which I pick, it will be the slowest. I thank the marketing gurus for impulse buying. Those trinkets buy my daughter's interest just long enough for me to make it through the line.

Unlike my offspring, dazzled by Chiclets and brica-brac, I listen to the people in front of me. One day, the woman in line before me had an infinite number of canned goods she was unloading from her buggy one at a time. The cashier looked at her and asked, "How are you?"

"Fine" the lady replied.

Neither made eye contact. It wasn't a real answer or question. The cashier continued to swipe can after can, and the woman continued to look harried and slightly forgetful.

Finally, I arrived in my place to be rung up. I was already wrung out, if you will pardon the play on words. The cashier asked, "How are you?"

I responded, "I'm tired. It's been a long day."

She said, "Me too, I've been here since 5:30 in the morning." It was now 5:00 P.M.

We began to talk about life's weariness and the joys of peace and rest. Before long she had my produce appropriately scanned and paid for. I got about twelve steps away and she said, "Get some rest."

I smiled back at her and nodded my head.

That's a picture of discipleship. It can be an emotionless exchange without any real connection, or it can bring life to the suffering. The only difference is connection. The tools and suggestions I use only point to a way to engage teenagers where they are. It helps me recognize them as God's works of art. You can do exactly the same thing if you will just be willing to connect.

Leading

Most young adults already want to connect. That's the good news. You walk into a relationship with a teen with a great opportunity. They need to feel connected. Deep inside them, they need to find their place in society. It's rooted in their identity. You will have the opportunity to build them up, encourage them, show them their significance, and reveal their connection to Christ.

The bad news in connecting them to all this is that you have to be willing to do that yourself. The ceiling on your ability to lead revolves around your experiences. It may sound like discipleship is geared toward older people. Not necessarily. Experiences can be collected by young and old. It's when and how you connect with your experiences that count.

You can't lead teenagers where you haven't gone yourself. If you tend to shy away from deeper conversations or hard decisions, you will have limited experiences in helping adolescents choose a harder road.

Discipleship is hard. It asks a person to be willing to change into a completely different version of himself. It's a better, more godly version; but it still a calls for change.

When I was newly married and living in Tennessee, I decided to get a dog. Some people would just go down to the pound or a pet store. Not me. I got several books and did the research. I didn't want a really big dog or one that sheds a lot or a little one that would bark in frequencies known to cause insanity. As my choices narrowed, I found that I was looking for a dog in the Terrier family. I finally settled on a Welsh Terrier.

The only problem now was finding one. The closest breeder I could find was over four hours away. So one Saturday in the beginning of October, I made the journey to check out this possible pet.

When I talked to the breeder, he confessed that he was really a Jack Russell breeder. If I had any doubt about that, it was dispelled when I pulled up several hours later. There were probably 2 million Jacks running around, trying their best to get my attention when I climbed out of my '87 GMC Jimmy. It felt like visiting an orphanage. They all wanted to go home with someone.

After finding the breeder and most of the dogs lost interest in me, we walked up a hill to a small kennel. Inside I found a wire hairball curled up in the corner. This was the Welshie. Staying out of the kennel, I walked around to try to get a better look at him. He teleported to the opposite side of the kennel whenever I approached. Ok, he was a little skittish.

Emboldened by my failure to start a friendship, I opened the kennel and walked in. The little guy rolled onto his back in the most submissive position he could find. I tried to get low, like all the books told me. Slowly, I reached out my hand to let him have an exploratory sniff. He peed himself and on me in the process.

No matter what I did, it was obvious that this dog was too scared to leave his kennel. He might have had an idea that something better was out there, but his fear kept him from it. I left without a dog. It was one of the most disappointing experiences I've had. Here I was trying to bring this dog into a new life, a better life, and he just couldn't see that better life.

Failing to connect resembles my experience with the Welsh Terrier. If you don't connect in a way that shows something better, you won't get very far. The best way to show that kind of life is by having one yourself. I'm not talking about an easier life or a more popular life. Just a better life.

Implementation

Practicing the ideas in this book may seem overwhelming. In presentations I've given, someone always asks, "How do I do all this?" It seems like taking golf lessons where the coach tells you address the ball, keep your head down, have a sitting posture, don't bend your arms, swing like a gate, relax your grip, hit past the ball, and connect. No human being can think of all that minutiae at once.

Many people after assimilating these ideas don't make big changes in the way they work with students. Ideas take some time to germinate, but they do grow eventually. If any of the practices caught your attention, you will likely start using them without thinking about it. Other times a situation will remind you of something and jog a memory.

If you want to be more proactive, try using one of these ideas at a time. Just like the golf lesson, you probably can't think of more than one at a time anyway (I certainly can't). Over time, you won't have to, though. Much of these tools developed over time for me. I don't actively think about them unless I find a challenging situation.

Process

In Chapter 2, the process of discipleship moves to the forefront of discipleship. The reason behind this shift is clear. Outcomes can't dominate a relationship without reducing it to an agenda. The danger in only considering the process comes in missing direction. While the process remains important, it can't live without direction.

Consider this. Teenagers often hang out with their friends. They have no outside objectives. They just want to have fun and maybe fill that sense of belonging. Without direction, discipleship is just like a hangout. Emphasis on the process only serves to keep an agenda out. The task then becomes to help a student find God's direction and point to that.

Dynamic

Having a dynamic relationship takes the process of discipleship and gives it direction. Caution should be taken in giving direction. Too often, if you come into a meeting with a canned set of goals, you will not be able to see any other options.

Being dynamic means you are watching for God to reveal himself and his plan in that meeting. This doesn't mean that you don't prepare. Instead the preparation changes. Instead of preparing a lesson plan, you have to prepare yourself. All of your presuppositions about an adolescent have to be unloaded.

I often pray for my will to be free and my heart to be open. While praying, I think about the person or people I am going to meet. What is happening in his life? What do I know about him? As my conversation with God continues, I ask God to fill in all the things that I don't know when we meet.

Heuristic

Building autonomy in discipleship only comes from setting aside your outcomes and leaning into a dynamic relationship. As freedom and autonomy develop, confidence will fill in the gaps left behind from a pre-planned encounter.

Heuristic leading can be a bit tricky. Too much freedom can become enabling of some bad behaviors. You will need to find a personal balance to allow the kind of autonomy that will be effective. If you've been able to set aside your own goals and listen, then you should be able to suggest some kind of response. Hold these suggestions lightly. If a student brushes them off, don't take it personally. Move on to something else, but keep up the expectation that change is welcome.

Specific

At this point in discipleship, you should have built some trust. That connection with a teen gives you some grace to start being very specific in what you see. It sometimes will be hard to give and to hear. Because of this possible tension, you need to rely on the student's autonomy.

Language becomes extremely important here. Telling a student they need to do something will crush autonomy. Instead, you might say, "I wonder what it would be like if you..." or "Have you considered..." This might sound a bit therapeutic to you, but there's a reason for this. It works. This kind of language keeps your personal goals out of the picture.

Personal

As you have already read, being specific isn't enough. You will have to be personal in discipleship to help teenagers. It's risky, but inevitable if you want to help them see themselves through God's eyes. The risk comes from revealing too much, too soon.

I have sometimes waited years before being able to bring up something personal with a teenager. Patience gets better with practice, though. The hardest part of being personal comes from students. Many times they will ask for personal feedback. You need to be absolutely sure they really want it before plunging into their lives.

Value

Value comes into play more as a diagnostic than a technique. As you allow for, and encourage, a teenager to have the freedom to set goals, you will need to help them see better goals than they already have. Any goal they set for themselves that hinges on external outcomes will eventually come to a dead end.

When a young adult reaches this place, usually the best thing you can do is ask, "Why?" If they want to be an artist, ask them why. If they want to go to college, ask them why. Your work in helping them realize values lies in finding their source.

Implicit

Chapter 8 is the hardest tool and the easiest to misuse. Most people naturally use implicit language in most of their friendships. At best, it helps their friends move past barriers, but more often it becomes a method for abuse. Control and manipulation are the two biggest dangers.

When using deliberate, implicit language, make sure you have spent enough time giving autonomy and freedom. Trust is paramount in giving implied messages. If at some point it becomes guilt producing or controlling, you will have abused your trust and severely damaged your relationship.

Last Words

As you might have seen, the chapters in the book are laid out in a progressive manner. They build into a deeper groove as you follow them down the path. You will likely start just trying to get to know someone and giving up your outcomes. That will easily bring you to a more dynamic relationship. You can use these out of sequence, but you will likely find yourself naturally doing them in a certain order.

You won't always need to be deliberate in the sequence of these suggested tools for discipleship. Often, after using them, you will use them without even thinking about it. Other times, you might need to take a little time to think through how to use them, especially with external values and implicit language.

Discipling teenagers will never be described as easy. I return to my original analogy. The best we can hope for in working with young people is to point to Jesus and allow him to do his work among them. Hopefully these prompts will help you in that endeavor. As you practice them, be God's workmanship, God's masterpiece.

End Notes

1. Leonardo da Vinci, The Notebooks of Leonardo Da Vinci, Complete (Library of Alexandria Press, 2003), Kindle location 1148.
2. Steve Jobs, *Think Different* (Apple Advertising Campaign, 1997)
3. Michael Frost and Alan Hirsch, *The Shaping of Things to Come: Innovation and Mission for the 21st-Century* (Grand Rapids, MI: Baker Books, Reprint edition, 2004), 14.
4. David E. Fitch, *The Great Giveaway: Reclaiming the Mission of the Church from Big Business, Parachurch Organizations, Psychotherapy, Consumer Capitalism, and Other Modern Maladies* (Grand Rapids, MI: Baker Books, 2005), 34-35.
5. John Eldredge, *Waking the Dead: The Glory of a Heart Fully Alive* (Nashville, TN: Thomas Nelson, 2006), 1-2.
6. Kinnaman, David, *You Lost Me: Why Young Christians Are Leaving Church...and Rethinking Faith* (Grand Rapids, MI: Baker Books, 2011), Kindle location 155-157.
7. Mike King, *Presence-Centered Youth Ministry: Guiding Students into Spiritual Formation* (Westmont, IL: IVP Books, 2006), 82.
8. Andrew Root, *Revisiting Relational Youth Ministry: From a Strategy of Influence to a Theology of Incarnation* (Westmont, IL: IVP Books, 2007), Kindle locations 111-113.
9. Eugene Peterson, *The Jesus Way: A Conversation on the Ways That Jesus Is the Way* (Grand Rapids, MI: Wm. B. Eerdmans Publishing Company; Reprint edition, 2011),
10. Donald Miller, *Blue Like Jazz: Nonreligious Thoughts on Christian Spirituality* (Nashville, TN: Thomas Nelson, 2003), ix.
11. Kinnaman, Kindle location 147-151.
12. Ken Robinson, *The Element: How Finding Your Passion Changes Everything* (New York, NY: Penguin Books,

2009), Kindle location 3457-3460.

13. Daniel H. Pink, *Drive: The Surprising Truth About What Motivates Us* (Riverhead Trade, 2011), Kindle location 389-392.

14. Pink, Kindle location 466-468.

15. George Santayana, *The Sense of Beauty* (CreateSpace Independent Publishing Platform, 2011),18.

16. Dieter Rams, BrainyQuote.com, http://www.brainyquote.com/quotes/quotes/d/dieterrams174975.html.

17. Jacques Barzun, *The Energies of Art* (London, England: Vintage, 1962), 332.

18. Albert Camus, *Notebooks 1935-1951* (Portland, OR: Marlowe & Co, 1998), 33.

19. Francis Schaeffer, *The Francis A. Schaeffer Trilogy: The Three Essential Books in One Volume* (Wheaton, IL: Crossway, 1990), 94.

20. D. A. Carson, *A Call to Spiritual Reformation: Priorities from Paul and His Prayers* http://www.monergism.com/thethreshold/articles/onsite/prayerchangesthings.html (June 1, 1992).

21. Mihaly Csikszentmihalyi, *Flow: The Psychology of Optimal Experience* (New York: NY: Harper Perennial; 1991), 6.

22. Ivon Chouinard, *Let My People Go Surfing: The Education of a Reluctant Businessman* (New York, NY: Penguin Books, 2006), Kindle location 923.

23. Patrick Rothfuss, *The Wise Man's Fear: The Kingkiller Chronicle, Day Two* (New York, NY: Penguin Group, DAW Trade, 2012), Kindle location 5083-5084.

24. Alice Meynell, *The Colour of Life* (Whitefish, MT: Kessinger Publishing, 2004), 1-2.

25. Madeleine L'Engle, *Many Waters* (New York: NY: Square Fish, Macmillan, 2007), Kindle location, 3956.

26. Paul Watzlawick, *The Language of Change: Elements of Therapeutic Communication* (New York, NY: W. W. Norton & Company, 1993), 85.

27. Watzlawick, 88.

28. Neil Gaiman, *Stardust* (New York, NY: William Morrow, 2012), Kindle location 3587.

29. Chip Heath and Dan Heath, *Switch: How to Change Things When Change Is Hard* (New York, NY: Crown Business, 2010), 6.

30. Heath, 8.
31. Weder, Heinz, *Der Makler* (Kandelaber Verlag Bern, 1969)
32. Patrick Rothfuss, *The Name of the Wind: Kingkiller Chronicles, Day One* (New York, NY: Penguin Group, DAW Trade, 2009), 658.
33. J. R. R. Tolkein, *The Fellowship of the Ring* (New York, NY: Ballantine Books, 1967), 224.

Art Notes

Cover Image
Water Lillies
http://commons.wikimedia.org/wiki/File:Monet_Waterlilypond_1926.jpg

Introduction
Mona Lisa
http://commons.wikimedia.org/wiki/File:Mona_Lisa,_by_Leonardo_da_Vinci,_ from_C2RMF_retouched.jpg

Chapter 1
Samurai
http://commons.wikimedia.org/wiki/File:Samurai_(1).jpg

Chapter 2
Monet's Church in Vetheuil
http://commons.wikimedia.org/wiki/File:Monet_-_Kirche_von_Vetheuil.jpg

Chapter 3
Joshua Reynolds The Strawberry Girl
http://commons.wikimedia.org/wiki/File:The_Strawberry_Girl_by_Joshua_ Reynolds.jpg

Chapter 4
Luis Melendez Still Life with Tomatoes a Bowl of Aubergines and Onions
http://commons.wikimedia.org/wiki/File:Still_Life_with_Tomatoes_a_Bowl_ of_Aubergines_and_Onions.jpg

Chapter 5
Johannes Vermeer The Astronomer
http://commons.wikimedia.org/wiki/File:Johannes_Vermeer_-_The_Astrono- mer_-_WGA24685.jpg

Chapter 6
Van Gogh The Portrait of Dr. Gachet
http://commons.wikimedia.org/wiki/File:Portrait_of_Dr._Gachet.jpg

Chapter 7
Caravaggio Doubting Thomas
http://commons.wikimedia.org/wiki/File:Caravaggio_Doubting_Thomas.jpg

Chapter 8
Renoir Bal du moulin de la Galette
http://commons.wikimedia.org/wiki/File:Pierre-Auguste_Renoir,_Le_Moulin_de_la_Galette.jpg

Chapter 9
Munch The Scream
http://en.wikipedia.org/wiki/File:The_Scream.jpg#filelinks